RANT
& Rhyme

Jesse Gonzalez Jr.

Published by

Dolphin Star

Copyright © 2019 by Jesse Gonzalez Jr.

All rights reserved.

ISBN: 978-0-9827408-2-8

To my kids, Jesse, Angelique and Abigail, for the crazy adventures your crazy dad took you guys on, and the memories you made with me. You are beautiful always.

To my mother Virginia. Thank you for standing by me through thick and thin and never giving up on me and being the hero always.

To the friends, family and people who inspired me to dream and cry and laugh and struggle and the one person out there who still holds my heart. No matter the roads we took , I will always love you and thank you for burning a fire in me.

Also would like to thank all those little trolls and lazy smooches and fat balding "friend zone," girlfriend-stealing, backstabbing ex-buddies. Big thumbs up for the material. May you happily grow fatter and balder to where you resemble a Mexican George 'the animal' Steele, "homie."

Contents

Foreword	i
Prologue	iv

Chapter 1 - Somber - 1

Lost In Your Moment	2
Your Smile	4
Get Away	6
What Will You Miss About Me When I'm Gone?	8
Fate	10
Forget Me Not	12
Faded	14
Finish My Dream For Me	16
Famous Or Infamous	18
My Year	20
Luv 2 Luv U	22
Do Unto Others	24
3230 S. Half Moon	26
I Hate Me	28
Capture	30
Breakthrough	32
In A Dream	34
I'm a Fool	36
Got It Bad	38
Broken 3	40
I Love Haters	42

Til Your Mine...Again	44
My First Last Love	46
My Child	48
Bring The Pain	50
I Will	52
Tu Carino	54
" "	56
No Excuses	58
Craving On You	60
Santa Monica	62
Far Gone	66
Rumble In My Heart	68
Eternal	70
McFarland	72
2nd Time Around	74
"40"	76
Boy Becomes The Man	78
The Hurt	80
Mother	82
Dreams	83
Bro	84
Sick And Tired Of Being Sick And Tired	88
If I Could	90
Honey	92
4 ½ Years	93
Bad EX'perience	96
Till We Meet Again	98
Fucking Hate That I Still Fucking Love You	100

I Am What I Am	102
Hellish Life	104
Rewind	106
Unapologetic	108
Gone 4 Good	110
The Writer	112
No Fame	114
Dark Times	116
Things Left Unsaid	119
F(aith) You	121
2208	123
Hard To Love	125
The Note	127
Wordz	129
I Wish	131

Chapter 2 - Awakenings - 133

So N2U	134
Inspire My Fire	137
Life's Great	139
Ellington	141
She Didn't Have To	143
I Am	145
The Promise	147
My Greatest Love	149
Her	151
Frankenstein Heart	153
When I Die	155

Baby Girl	158
What If	160
Spellbound	162
12/6	164
Birthdays	166
Invisible Walls	169
Let Sleeping Demons Lay	171
Gold	173
Fakebook	175
Nuthin Else Matterz	178
Madre	181
Graveyard Of Broken Hearts	183
After The Fall	185
Created To Be Hated	187
Battlefield	189
Mirror, Mirror	191
Smile	193
Raise My Fist	195
On The Real	197
If You Ever Have Forever In Mind	199
Glimmer and Fade	201
Two Little Girls	203
#NOTENOUGHHOURS	205
Thorns	207
Music	209
Oh Sister	211
Angies 20th B-day	213

Lifetime	214
Hey Dad	216
Woke	218
Fieldworker's Son	219

Chapter 3 - Woke - 220

Writers Block	222
She Is	224
Broken Man	226
Live For The Memories	228
Can't Sleep	230
Mama Cried	231
Queen	234
Random	236
When I'm Gone	237
Toxic People	239
Fools Gold	241
Backseat	243
Father's Day	246
I Remember...	248
Oh My Brother	250
Tidal Wave	252
Sacred	254
One Day	256
Kingdom	258
#Fuckit	260
The Year	262
Wish I Never Knew	264

Book Of You	267
Lost	269
Beautiful Day	271
Villain	273
After The Fall pt2	275
One Thing	277
Wannabe	278
Battered	280
Last Day On Earth	282
She's Gone	284
Here Lies A Man	286
Girl With The Broken Smile	288
Just Saying	291
Feel It	293
Paisa	295

Foreword

A psychologist named Howard Gardner believed that human intelligence is comprised of 8 different types. One of these intelligences is known as emotional intelligence. Individuals who are higher than average in emotional intelligence are known to be and/or feel quite lonely throughout their lives.

The reason for this is because, while these individuals might be very accurate in knowing exactly how and why they are feeling the way they do, they don't have a way of sharing those well-understood feelings with others. By expressing such precise feelings of despair or anguish to the average person, they might feel that they will scare others off. They may seem intimidating by coming off as too intense. Thankfully, those with this degree of emotional intelligence are often understood by expressing themselves another way – like poetry for example.

The author has created this book as a means to be understood both by himself and by others. It isn't easy to put life events into spoken words, but when you put a pen to paper, it often seems like the poem writes itself, especially if you're in the throes of despair.

What was once an intangible, incoherent mess of noises, slurs, and curses soon become rhymes, and alongside it, a hope to become understood in a world that is often misunderstanding.

Humans were not meant to walk through this world alone, but by you reading this poem, you can be one more person who understands another, if only a little more. Like you, this author has gone through some tough times (to say the least) and also, moments that I am sure he would not trade the world for.

I assisted the author in preparing this book, and I have seen that each writing you are about to read contains a pure, raw, unadulterated description of what he was feeling and going through at the time.

Some authors may hold back, because they feel like they have some reputation to uphold, but such considerations are not taken here.

This book was written by a fighter with an interesting record – someone who lost many battles, won few, but who is still moving forward anyway.

This book was written by someone who has struggled their whole life, who is used to getting their hands dirty even though his last visit to urgent care urged him to rest more. This book was written by someone who is no stranger to pain, and though many have heard him speak, few have truly listened.

But most importantly, this book was written by someone who has been there for me throughout my whole life…this book was written by my father.

- Jesse Isaac Gonzalez

Prologue

Here you are holding in your hands my second book, my baby, ten years in the making.

This book does not only focus on my past relationships but also my children and my relationship with them. My first book dwells on my stress in life, such as maintaning stressful jobs, losing them, losing my mom and dad, and losing other family members and friends. This book will take you much deeper into my life and feelings, for example the loss of my father, and the dealing with the demons that drove me to attempt suicide and failing to do so.

It also shows the happy moments in my life: my love of music, celebrating the sucesses of even small life improvements, and just crazy shit, like dreams or simply the way I look at life.

Finally this book tells of my total inspiration in God through thick and thin, happiness and sorrow.

This book offers a journey through my crazy, twisted life and all its moments through my urban-poem rhymes as only I can tell. And no, I'm not playing the little victim role either, so chill, you trolls!

Some of these poems just describe heartbreak and betrayal, happiness and love, all at random, just because I feel like describing the feeling. I in no way aim to hurt anyone. I don't even drop a single name.

If anyone out there finds offense in what I write, by all means write your own book and throw me under the bus as well then put that bitch in reverse and run me over again! Freedom of speech, baby! I'm not hurting anyone, just expressing what I want. As I say on my social media outlets, "If you don't like what I'm saying, fuck! Keep scrolling!"

In my case I just decided to rant and rhyme. Thats all. If you like it thank you. If you don't, hey by all means go fuck yourself.

Just kidding!

Do as I do: give everything a chance in life, people, movies, books, love, God, even your enemies.

Thats what Rant and Rhyme means.

Chapter 1

Somber

The following rhymes are based a relationship that lasted four and a half years of marriage that introduced me to being a born again Christian. It eventually ended after many false restarts, and proved hopeless with a bitter divorce.

I will remember the good times though as I do in all my failed relations. It is, however, the somber memories, that fire up my inspiration for these rhymes.

Lost In Your Moment

Sometimes I get lost in a daze.
I admire over you as you sleep,
Touch your angel like face.
Where did you come from?
How did you pull me in this deep?
You are everything I have always wanted.
Can this be so true?
I've been to every club.
Every party, looking for a woman like you.
Seems like God answered my hopes
Cause here you are out of the blue,
There comes a moment when I cant let go.
There is a moment when I want to go slow.
There is a moment when I wish
I could give you the moon and stars,
But I wish for nothing to change,
Cause I love you the way you are.
I love the way you talk to me.
I get lost in your innocent like ways,
You are my wildest fantasy.
Then there is that certain way you make me feel.
You are in many ways like me.

I cant believe youre so real.
Just your mere touch makes me melt.
I'll never forget our first date,
The feeling is indescribable how I felt.
If every rainbow had a pot of gold,
I know this is the kind of love that can never feel old,
If every raindrop had a purpose,
I'd know that this life can revolve around us.
I wish I could fast forward
To the future of you and me.
Tto the part where I'm on bended knee.
I know this can happen soon to where im kissing you
And carrying you in my arms on our honeymoon.
This can happen I just know it.
Oh well, sometimes I just get carried away.
When im with you I just get lost in your moment..

Your Smile

Your smile can light up a room.
Not just my room but my world.
Not just my world but my galaxy.
But this is only a little of what you mean to me.
I've had a bad day and I'm angry and depressed.
My life is a blur and filled with so much stress.
Then you smile.
Everything I had to worry about now seems minimal,
All the hurt all the pain
All the worst now seems subliminal.
What is your message where is your hint?
You're still a mystery.
All this is so little of how much you mean to me.
You were worth the while.
All the searching, all the desperation,
All for your smile.
Your laughter brings life
Into what was once this dark soul.
With each passing day
I am for certain love you more.
Your innocent, shy grin that creeps from ear to ear.
I'm so lucky I have you.

I'm so lucky I am here.

Not only are you sexy and beautiful.

But you have a certain unique style.

You walk up to me and look into my eyes.

And then you smile,

And a certain tingle and vibration

Goes up and down my spine.

For every question deserves an answer.

Yor every rumble there is a rhyme.

That's your power that draws me closer.

That's your power

That makes angels dance on the moon.

You walked into my life.

You walked into my world.

Then you smile.

And you lit up my entire room...

Get Away

Lets get out and hit that open road.
Lets get in get on and move out, before we get old.
Let us both watch that sun set,
Ttalk about old times and the first time we met.
Lets just leave everything behind, no worries no stress
Just you and me and an open mind.
Call out any hotel get any old room,
Don't think of yesterday just today and tomorrow
And better days will be here soon.
As we count down the miles to our destination,
Doesn't matter where we end up
As long as I have your full attention.
Lets drink margaritas and roll around on the beach.
Better memories and wild dreams are within reach.
The glistening of your skin, your laughter,
And your dark sunglasses and your hair in the wind,
Holding your hand as we shop from store to store,
I am reassured this is why I need you in my life.
Everyday, more and more.
Holding you tightly around your waist.
Kissing you in public without a care.
I don't care if people stop and stare.

Let's go find the nearest bar.
We have no troubles, lets drink 'til dawn
At our own private wonderland that's never too far.
Waking up next to you, I treasure these moments
Because the hours are way too few.
It's time to pack and get back to our old life stye
When times get bad well just fly back to yesterday
Live in the moment, live for the time,
Live for another get away.

What Will You Miss About Me When I'm Gone?

What will you miss about me when im gone?
What is it, what will it be hun?
The raindrops tapping on your window sill?
The silence of the night, that quiet empty feel?
Would you look back in anger?
The big closet, but my side will only be an empty hanger.
The smell of my cologne, the sadness, the fear of being alone?
My babycakes, my sweetie pie, I wipe your face
As I watch a tear roll down the corner of your eye.
The warmth of my body, my lips on the back of your neck?
Man I always hated to see you upset.
Our walks underneath the moonlight?
Our laughter in the middle of the day?
Our love-making in the middle of the night?
Would you leave out all the bad parts
And just think of the good times?
Will it be hard to move on with your life
With me always on your mind?
The struggle of getting to where we were.
The longing, the dreams, always wanting more.
What will you miss? The security of a great lover.
Or the feel of my skin.

Missing out on an uncertainty with a trusting friend.
Will you always hold me in your highest regard?
Or will your feelings be bittersweet,
Painful to recall and much too hard.
Would you smile if you saw me out in public?
Would time stand still as the world rushed past us
In a blurring traffic?
Would every single minute, every movie, every song,
Just what would it be?
What will you miss about me when I'm gone?

Fate

I once gave up on love.
I was filled with so much hate,
Then one cool fall day I walked out
And walked right into fate.
Who knows what God has in plan,
I was so broken down,
Only half a man.
Laughing on the outside,
Tortured and beaten on the inside,
I buried my face in my hands.
All those tears I fought.
I must've been the last person on earth
Who love forgot I guess.
I would sit it out and wait,
Til one fall day…fate.
You pulled me out
When I was at the bottom of this dark abyss
You're everything I have lost,
Everything in my life I have missed.

I was laying in a pool of my own sorrow,
Moping around in anger,
Living for the day
And not even living for tomorrow.
I was at the end of my rope.
God gave me light.
He gave me you
And you gave me hope.
Just when I thought it was too late.
One cool fall day, fate.
I thank God you found me,
I was tired of feeling the company of misery,
Nothing to look forward to but an empty room,
Quiet fights with my demons
And my own near doom.
But now that old life ends,
A fresh start, a new chapter,
A new life with you begins.
I still have my problems and sleeping demons.
But now they are easily ignored.
My heart feels strong
Because I feel loved and adored.
Like a needle in a giant haystack
I have found my soulmate.
All because of one cool fall day,
I went to work and later walked right into...fate.

Forget Me Not

From the minute we first met
I knew we would connect with your very first step.
Do you recall what we would go on
To create with our first meeting that fall.
Our love was so new born,
We were both hungry to grow,
So anxious to learn.
You were so young and afraid of the world.
You told me I was yours and you wanted to grow old.
And even when your family ignored you
And you were shunned.
After all the wars we fought,
Forget me not.
I was your fool, I was your clown
Always quick to bring you up and reverse that frown.
Believe me when I say all is forgiven.
You were worth every memory.
We both have a lot of living.
Even now when I am just an afterthought,
Forget me not.
When the rain is dancing on your roof
And the cold wind hugs your face

If you listen closely you'll hear our laughter
Somewhere in your place.
And when you are in the arms of someone else,
Don't just think of me when all else fails.
When all else goes from cold to hot,
Forget me not.
And when you find yourself crying
In the middle of the night,
Because of things you regret,
Somewhere under the same moon,
I'll still be thinking of you
Because I'll never forget.
In time all this will pass,
And you will succeed in life and gain a whole lot.
When this does, forget me not.
In the meanwhile
Don't despair,
Wipe your tears and smile.
You have the will to hold on and fight.
You know at the end of your tunnel there is always light.
Always believe don't give up so easily
In what you can achieve,
And in the end when you think all is lost.
Always trust in God,
And forget me not.

Faded

True love broken.
Words thought of but never spoken.
Tears shed, finding the courage,
Finding the right words but never said.
My hands caressing your face.
The flow of your silky black hair,
Im with you at the moment,
But really not there.
Total silence after our dispute,
You and I can apologize,
But we both refuse.
In the still of the night,
The creaking of the house,
What we could've been
If we did what was right.
Words at the tip of our tongue,
Empty space on the wall
Where our wedding picture once hung.
The sinking of your heart,
Not wanting to be where you're at every single minute.
Every single second growing further apart .

Laying motionless on the bed, facing each other
Wanting so bad to read whats going through your head..
Tears rolling down your cheek.
Your lips quiver as you find the courage to speak.
Afraid of tomorrow, even more scared
Of living in a world of lonliness and sorrow.
Your expression gives away all your doubt,
Finding the strength to remain calm
When all you wanna do is shout.
Feels like I've learned to read you like a diary from a page
From your book, felt like I was in the middle
Of an earthquake.
Everything around me stood still
But I was the only one who shook..
Your silence says a million words
That could almost roll out of your lips.
I don't know if im dreaming
Or has my reality just slipped?
Holding on to something that is long gone,
Not knowing what you did in the past to change.
What did you do that was so wrong?
True love that you once upon a time you couldn't forget,
Fading slowly and quickly turning to resent.
Holding out for hope, for you to just say it.
Not wanting to live another day
Empty hurt, and just faded.

Finish My Dream For Me

Dear son, I write this with a positive vibe.
If anything should happen, always remember
I lived a blessed life.
But I had a vision the other day,
If for some unknown reason
I would not see my work succeed
Because I would not finish my story
Despite everything ive ever done,
I'd be happy and thankful to the good Lord
If He were to call and I would be gone.
Just the other day I had a dream.
I was talking to the good Lord over coffee and cream,
We spoke about everything at random.
Everything that was going on in my world and then some.
Never in my life did I ever get so much insight.
Like I could never go back and undo my wrongs,
But live my life now and keep doing things right.
From here on out, I need to finish my projects.
I want people to know what I was really about.

My struggles my tears, my dreams, my private fears.
Even if this don't ever make me rich,
Just to see the lives it would touch,
And the lessons it would teach,
I don't care how long the process takes.
Some days I feel like my dream is within reach.
I feel the song in my heart.
I feel the good Lord on my shoulder
Even when I'm falling apart.
Dear son, I need you to understand this labor of love,
I need you to finish this dream for me.
If I'm ever called from up above.
There is so much power in my pen,
Even when your heart is closed
Its always important to keep your mind open.
Always have the power to discuss,
Always to keep your views and never lose focus.
After I finished my conversation with my good Lord,
I thought about when stuff goes wrong,
I'll go back to this day
Beacuase His promise is embedded in my head
Down to every single word.
This is where I need to be,
This is what I want the world to see.
Don't let me go undone.
Finish my dream for me.

Famous Or Infamous

I will never forget where I came from
As a kid I worked the dirt fields under the hot sun.
Never say I am a stranger to hard work.
You can only push me so far before I can become a jerk
I am proud to say, I am proud to be,
I've got Mexican American blood instilled
And running through me..
So natural of everything that makes up J-E double S-E
Yes I am the oldest of Jesus and Virginia,
I love those old folks but its been so long since I seen ya.
I'm immune to gossips and my worst critic
What you see is what you get I don't have to hide it.
Some may say im a loser,
I know I am not a habitual womanizer drug abuser
Or daily boozer.
I've got a habit where I usually offend.
Don't be afraid there is a message I intend to send.
Don't have the biggest house or a large bank account
But I do have God I am so glad He is the one I found.
Never cared to much for the bright lights of the fame.
I am more content on writing a book
And leaving behind a mark emblazoned with my name.

I've learned any fool can make a baby,
But it takes a real man to raise one.
I am proud to have brought up two daughters and a son.
Don't need to get into a fight to call myself a man.
I'd pick a flower for my lady
And get down on one knee to show who I really am.
I'll cry at a chick flick.
I hold true hate for men who prey on children,
That just makes me sick.
I live my days like if they were my last.
But I don't take life for granted
Cause any minute I could go really quick and fast.
Live every second to the fullest.
I may never be rich but I'll be happy
When the day comes that I'm laid to rest.
Glory be to the highest, I may have stumbled but in the end
I know I passed every test.
Im gonna be famous or infamous.
I never did more but never settled for less.

My Year

I was like a fighter in into the 12th round.
And I was all but knocked out.
Then you came along and I was found.
After all the torment, all my anguish, all those tears.
I told myself next time around its gonna be my year.
Yes I do remember hitting pay dirt.
All those sirens in my head, going off like red alert.
I almost threw in the towel.
I was bitter, angry, couldn't stop crying foul.
So glad I didn't admit defeat.
Would've missed out on chance when you and I
Would finally get a chance to meet.
So excited to be here, this time around…my year.
Don't tell me I should be feeling guilty.
Where were you when you didn't need me?
Don't say im living in sin,
when you didn't even care to see how I've been..
I'm blessed for what I've done.
Im even more thankful for who I've become.
You didn't see me hanging by a string.
My entire life hanging in the balance.
Almost lost faith in God, love, and romance.

Almost fell into that abyss.

Don't be critical.

Where were you when my life was a total mess..

I'm strong where I stand.

My heart still bleeds and I still got the scars on my hand.

Time to put this train back on track.

The dare to dream express is out on the attack.

My future is so bright I have to squint.

So glad I didn't give up, so glad I didn't quit.

So glad I didn't disappear.

This time around it's my year!

Luv 2 Luv U

This is you, this is us.
Everything that was once negative is now in the past.
Everything we have now is surely a plus.
Have you ever been awoken from a dream as you sleep?
When you wake do you still think your dreaming
Or am I just falling in love deep?
That's the way I feel when im around you.
The way some women are now so little so few.
All grown up now, I know what I want.
No need to show off
Got nothing to flaunt.
Tired of the clubs.
Tired of the chase.
I'm in love with your body, I'm in love with your soul.
I'm in love with your face.
Poets are like porn stars.
We both bare all.
Im as certain in love like after the summer then comes fall.
Like after the dawn, theres the morning dew.
Like in the way I feel when I love to love you.

And if ever you should leave,
On this bed of nails I will wait.
You are worth it when you bring me happiness
And erase all my prior hate.
I welcome the troubled times.
But I also treasure when we think with the same open minds.
I want to make it like a fairy tale.
I don't want to quit.
I just want to try harder when all else fails.
I can be your Prince Charming, a new day is upon us.
A second wind, a second coming.
I want to make it look like in a Disney cartoon.
Carry my princess on my white horse
And fly you off to the moon.
I want to look at fifty years from now
At how it all began and how it grew.
But most of all I want to continue
To love to love you.

Do Unto Others

Jesus Christ I been through hell,
So damn tired of the same story,
But I get myself inspired to tell.
I know you've got a plan for me.
I know there is a reason for the pain, the agony.
The let downs, month after month year after year
And season after season..
Wake up every morning, and just go to work.
I'm tossed around throughout the day
But I get stronger with every single jerk..
You can put a band aid on a cut,
But not on my heart.
I start every day like a fresh new start.
Your unselfish ways are the reasons why im still here.
The unpredictability of life is the only thing I fear.
It took a lot to happen for me to awaken.
Everything I ever owned was suddenly taken.
Thank you Lord, they came and took my car.
Thank you Lord, I closed my eyes
And whished upon a fallen star

My whole life is now in complete sabotage.
Thank you Lord I can see what happens
Ahead of me, or is that a mirage?
My faith is strong with you Lord Christ.
I'll shed my blood out on the battlefield
Until I earn my stripes.
Ill fall to my knees as I fight temptation.
I'll heed your calling when the time comes
Without hesitation..
I'll hold you in the highest honor,
Even to you the Son, the Holy Spirit
And the Holy Father.
For I am the reason you wear that crown of thorns
For you are the reason I was simply born.
The world can continue to spit on me.
Laugh behind my back, relish in my misery.
All this to me, it no longer bothers.
Ill just look up at the sky and smile
As I continue to do unto others.

3230 S. Half Moon

It began so much like a fairy tale.
We were brought together by fate.
We came from pasts that were hell.
I know there was something there.
I know there was.
Could it have been too much?
Too fast? For this sudden loss?
I don't know if its too late to go back,
But anything would be better than us being mad.
We were like two strangers locked up in a room.
Such sadness and heartbreak at 3230 South Half Moon.
A bed of roses, a beautiful blue sky.
I take one look at you and I too sigh.
You are everything I have ever searched for.
Wou are immaculate down to the last detail and more.
You are what I desire.
You make me go all night.
Wou make me start the fire.
So what then does this bring?
We fight over one tiny flaw
And all of a sudden it changes everything I know.

I can be hard to understand.

I try to be the best but at the end I am just a man.

But all we shared came from within.

And was so true.

Such compromise, such hardship on 3230 South Half Moon.

So what then shall the stars reveal?

You are the only woman that I love that is so real.

So what then do the heavens hold?

Your jealousy and insecurity make you look so cold.

There are other people in my life I cannot forget.

I made this clear the first day we met.

I need to be a father first, and a lover second.

You need to understand this in order for us to make it.

Please don't make me choose.

I see in us a future, but if Im forced to decide we both lose.

I don't want to say it was too fast, too soonl.

I don't want to say triumph and tragedy

At 3230 South Half Moon.

I Hate Me

Been feeling like an unfinished tattoo.
No color no fade, lines not connected.
Same old nothing new.
Too many negative people in my past life infected.
I try to enjoy my new life to ease the pain a lot faster.
But I cant erase the mistakes or people in my past
Who live among me like cancer.
Being unemployed really bites,
Not knowing when your next dollar is coming
Brings many sleepless nights.
What I would give to be younger.
I'd correct my wrongs,
I'd have the will, the fire, the drive,
I'd have the hunger.
But I wear my mistakes like a badge of honor.
I don't regret becoming wiser,
A son, a brother, a lover, a father.
Yet I cant help but mask my pain
From the people I love today.
Everyday is the same,
The sadness doesn't leave no matter hard I pray.

Time seems to be my worst enemy.

Cant change what can't be changed.

Just get older.

God, I hate me.

Being labeled loser seems to be my only destiny.

God, I hate me.

My daughters seem to have erased me from their memory

God, I hate me.

My enemies have gotten the last laugh more frequently.

God, I hate me.

Only my bills come calling lately.

God, I hate me.

Time to put my mask on and hide this face of misery.

I believe in God.

So why don't you envy me?

Capture

Isnt it funny how life is,
So full of the unexpected,
Sometimes sorrow and sometimes bliss.
Don't you wish you had a bottle
To capture all the finest moments in your life?
Growing up, school, your friends,
Even up to the moment you met your wife.
I wish I could go back in time
And capture my childhood.
I'd bottle it up and open it
Whenever I was in a bad mood.
The feeling of being careless and free,
No worries, no fear,
Just bursting with energy.
Running through an open field, chasing butterflies,
Rolling down a grassy hillside,
Giggling and laughing,
I wish I could still do that.
It would be nice.
Wish I could freeze the momen my children were born,
So I could shelter them from hardships, heartbreak.
And everything that later in life they would learn.

I would love to recapture innocence, and happiness,
I would bottle up true love, trust,
And the real meaning of life.
I must confess if I could wear magic sunglasses
And look back into my past,
Would I do everything right
To make a relationship last?
Or would I look deep into the future
To see what life would bring.
Nothing else matters
Because I've already captured today,
And today means everything.

Breakthrough

Daydream, believer, call me what you will,
You never had faith,
Your negativity is the only thing that kills.
Your patience was so little so few.
Couple years later look at me,
Breakthrough.
You laughed at my ideas.
You spat in my face.
Now all you see is my name up in lights,
My image all over the place.
You're probably ready to kick yourself
Asking yourself "Who knew?"
If only you had waited to see me
Breakthrough
All my work is of my blood.
My sweat and my tears.
Never lived for yesterday.
Never lived for tomorrow.
I only lived without fear.
Now look at me blasting off into the stratosphere.
Off into the sky so blue.
Breakthrough.

You shook your head, you rolled your eyes,
I put up with all your abuse and your mental lies.
My only relief was this paper and pen.
And many prayers to the good Lord.
Who would've believed people would be reading
About my experiences word for word?
So much I wanted you to believe.
So much I needed your support and all my feelings
And all my hurt I wanted you to absorb.
It seems like an over night sensation.
My name, my image, all across this nation
And even the world.
Heaven knows this all could've been yours
If you could've still been my girl.
All those lonely years, look at me now.
Breakthrough.
But it does get lonely in all these strange places/
No family, no loved ones, only different faces.
You sacrifice everything for success, love, home,
The place you grew.
You sacrifice everything for that one goal.
Breakthrough!

In A Dream

I died today, but you wouldn't know by looking at me.
I hurt in every inch of my body in every corner of my soul.
I even hurt in places I didn't even know.
Thought I heard your voice just the other day.
Could've been just a dream,
Or is my life just on time delay.
Thought I saw yourself in an apparition.
You looked so real, your movements,
But it was just my imagination.
I'm walking a fine line, Im fighting with my own past,
And fighting with my mind.
Don't know what part of myself to believe.
Im engulfed in an inferno of grief.
I'm burnt down to the core.
I dig deep til I cant find myself no more.
What is causing this affliction?
Sometimes I find myself happy and fine.
But I know that's just a contradiction.
I wish I could see the end
But my life gets too blurred that I get lost
That I don't know where to begin.

I'm in a dream, everyone is talking but sounding numb.
I'm moving in slow motion but I'm trying to run.
There is a lot of pointing fingers
Everyone is laughing at me,
Cold-hearted people, I don't know anyone;
Just a bunch of strangers.
I feel the earth underneath me tremble.
I see a reminder of us everyehere;
Every object, every symbol.
My feet are not even touching the ground.
I go through my day talking and yelling
Without even making a sound.
My body and bones pop, crackle, and snap,
Until I shatter, everyone looks down at me where I lay
Concerned, then they move away leaving me there
Like I don't even matter.
I'll awake from endless sorrow.
I get on my knees and just pray for a better tomorrow.
In the distance I hear a scream,
I look around and realize its me.
I thought I had awakened
But im back in a dream.

I'm a Fool

Sorry I broke your heart.
So much to say with so little time.
Don't know where to start.
You deserve better, I been trying to tell you.
I have such a hard time with words,
Should've left you a letter.
Sometimes I miss you so bad.
Other times, I'm so sick of you,
Because you make me so mad.
So many highs, so many things left unsaid.
I can't go to sleep with so many things running through my head.
It's all about you, it's all about us.
Maybe that's why I can't commit,
Can't deal with all the fuss.
It's all the finger pointing, all the drama.
Sometimes I wish I were dead or stuck in a coma.
Either way I don't regret meting you.
I wish I were the right person,
But I'm a fool.
You're beautiful and so giving inside and out.
I wish I was more like you.
But I'm still waiting for that person to one about.

I guess we lost too much inspiration I have yet to find.
Too busy fighting ghosts and demons and fighting my mind.
It would be unfair for you to wait.
I know sometime soon I'll be ready,
But by then it will be too late.
I do believe in hope.
If you must leave me, I've got the noose,
You can have the other end of my rope.
I'm not relationship material.
I wish you'd leave me for someone more deserving.
More surreal.
I'm not being negative.
Just didn't want to jump in this so quick.
I'm sorry for hurting you.
I'm sorry for being such a dick.
Please move on and leave me in my drowning pool.
At this moment I'm dangerous, not ready.
I'm a fool.

Got It Bad

You've got me so full of anticipation.
I get lost in your smile I lose concentration.
Yes I admit I got it bad for you.
Everything gets lost in translation,
I forget what to do.
You seem to walk on air,
You go through life like you haven't a care.
I been studying you and trying to analyze,
What can it be about you.
Could it be your attitude or how I drift away in your eyes?
Yeah, it gets to me just a little, just a tad.
Sometimes I hate to admit how much I got it bad.
And yes you're still a mystery.
A happy little girl on the outside,
But on the inside a sad beautiful lady.
But among all this confusion,
You're a breath of fresh air, a beautiful intrusion.
Just what makes me long for you when your not around?
Just what makes me jump in my car
To see you on the other side of town.
Just what is it about you that makes me understand
Just the sensuality I get from holding your hand.

You are everything beautiful that life brings.
You are the reason why the blue bird sings.
You make everything so much more clear,
And all this happens when you are with me,
Only when you are near.
I got to have you now, I gotta have you always.
I gotta have you here.
Wrapped tight around these strong arms,
Keeping you away from danger,
Keeping you away from all harm.=
You can be the best I ever had.
You are my medication for my ailment beacause I got it bad.

Broken 3

Met a girl but I broke her heart.
I thought she was the one.
Thought she was going to be my fresh start.
Baby I don't know exactly what went wrong.
Im just a broken man.
I cant exactly pinpoint my decision.
I just don't think you'll ever understand.
I'm sure you heard someone say on the rumor.
That kinda stuff always starts small, almost like a tumor.
That stuff always spreads like cancer.
People start to talk cause they have so many questions.
but no one has an answer.
But nobody has been through what I been through.
I don't think this relationship should pay for my mistakes.
Do you?
I know you think I just want to be free,
But what is freedom when the prison bars only exist in my head,
Too painful in my memory.
So much has passed, I'm not yet well.
I cant yet find my heaven,
when I'm still currently walking through my own hell.

Wish I would've met you a few years from now.
And not this quick.
I know I seem happy on the outside.
But from within I am far too sick.
You need to let me recover.
I ask of you for time and patience so I gain relief
and become a better friend and better lover.
I hate how we have this continuing war.
I continue to hurt you.
I'm trying to open your eyes.
That you don't deserve me anymore.
I'm tired of the lies, I'm tired of the fake smile.
I need to be alone so please give me space give me a while.
And if you should move on after I get better.
I would only shed a tear in my eye.
And a prayer in my heart, and thank God that I met her.
You brought inspiration and you brought light,
But no matter we couldn't pretend
Because my road wouldn't be paved.
It just wouldn't be right.
Unspoken.
Let's not say nothing more,
Til I piece myself together from being too far out;
More broken.

I Love Haters

I cant live my life.
I cant please everyone.
Cant live my day, cant have my day under the sun.
People will always talk no matter what you do.
I learned that the hard way.
There is always whispering, gossiping,
And believing in heresy.
You can do the world a lot of good,
That isn't entertaining enough.
People just insist on being rude.
Someone always has to be an instigator.
I just laugh and smile, I love haters.
There is always someone there
Who thinks they know more than you.
They hear something good about yourself
And they have to knock you down a peg or two.
They can't stand to see you succeed.
All that matters is how they think:
Pure selfish greed.
That's why I had to move away from my old town.
Just got tired of the phoniness
And the same people trying to tear me down.

Always trying to dig up something useless.

Something to make up.

Most times I get tired I just feel like telling them to fuck off.

People who you thought you knew

Turn out to just be traitors.

Take a deep breath, count to ten, and smile.

Gotta love my haters.

I divide myself from people who do the same old.

I just focus on forward and use them as a stepping stone.

I try not to look to my past, I try not to fall into their trap.

Whatever I did then, I moved on.

I could care less for their high school crap.

I got too much to live for.

I've already lost too much.

I gotta continue to live for me, and try to ignore.

You cant stop your life to satisfy everybody.

Its either now or later.

Just gotta shake my head and wave out to them

With my middle finger and think...I love my haters.

Til Your Mine...Again

Look up at the sky and count the stars.
I sometimes wonder where you are.
Seems like just yesterday,
Yet yesterday seems so far.
I wish I could move on so easy like you.
I wish I could spend a day in your shoes.
I wish I were stronger, I wish I was that kind.
Here's to wishful thinking, til your mine..again
My heart hurts with every single pump.
Some days I'm good
Other days I'm in my usual slump.
And its so hard for me after all those years
To think all I got was a broken heart as a souvenier.
And I try to do good,
But no matter how hard I try
Im always misunderstood.
Why does it look like everything you say and do
Looks so damn well?
Meanwhile here I sit in my own personal hell.

I ask God to help me stop being so bitter,
Angry and full of regret.
I have many issues im carrying,
Too many grudges that yet haven't left.
I used to be your knight in shining armor.
Now I have to sit back and see the pictures
On facebook and your new lover.
Where is that strength that I need to find?
I hate this feeling.
I hate this longing of hoping til your mine..again
The more I try the more I lose faith.
I never stop even in my darkest days,
And every little memory of you swirls
And fucks with my mind.
I should be moving forward
Instead I feel like im stuck in rewind.
Maybe til the end, maybe til I die,
Maybe til your mine …again.
And I don't even know why I obsess over you.
I thought my way finished, I thought we were through.
I know someday I'll be fine.
I'll be done thinking and hoping
Til your mine..again.

My First Last Love

You took my pain, you brought it to me.
You brought me pain, then you just left with just misery.
Could I fall in love again after being in love for so long?
Was I actually in love all this time
With the person I thought was right
When she was actually wrong?
My mind tells me no, my heart tells me yes.
We had plenty of good times
But the last few years were a mess.
Was all this just a fairy tale
That was supposed to end this way?
Was it supposed to start so pure, innocent,
And then end in disarray?
Now I cant get her out of my head,
She's moved along with someone else
And when I think of her all I see is red.
Should I do the same?
She's made it look so easy.
It's been almost two years, but I still go insane.
She was my first last love,
Is there someone out there?

I just cant take another heartbreak.

I had enough.

I can still recall the smell of her skin.

The color of her hair..

I reach out to touch her.

But next to me in bed is an empty space.

Theres no one there.

I keep wanting to wake up from this endless nightmare..

How much more can I take?

I've tried the dating scene.

But every girl I end up with makes me feel so fake.

She was the first girl I ever fell in love with.

She was the last to break my heart.

What is it about love?

Should I keep trying

Or have I had enough?

My Child

My dear child I write this to remind you.
That no matter where you go you will always carry a piece of me.
And that I will always love you more than you will ever know.
I was there for your birth.
I praised God and cried tears of joy
When you arrived here on this here earth.
Sit by myself and watch old videos of you.
My how you've grown over the years.
I laugh as you stumble and fall on my screen.
And out pour the tears.
Its not your fault that me and your mom never reconciled.
No matter where in this world you travel
You will always be my child.
You come and visit me on the weekend.
We have so much fun it saddens me when you leave.
I feel like I still envision you here and I have to pretend.
Where has the time gone?
I feel so much older watching my two daughters
And my only son.
I know somedays I may still sound hurt and full of anger.
But when you guys appear you soften my soul
And it makes me feel so much younger.

Im sorry if I ever did or said anything.
Its not my style.
Deep down I wish I could see you everyday,
Tuck you into bed and say a prayer together.
I just miss my child.
I daydream of seeing you soon again.
I will always be more than just your father.
I want to be your friend.
Your pictures adorn my wall.
I smile as a tear rolls down my cheek,
To know that not too long ago
You were just learning to crawl.
It hurts but it warms my heart when I see you smile,
Just to know that no man in this world has the prestige
Of calling you my child.

Bring The Pain

Please God help me erase this bitterness and hate.
Didn't know this was gonna be my new destination.
Didn't know this was gonna be my fate.
Once upon a time I had everything I ever wanted.
Now I'm left with emptiness
That makes me feel so hollow and haunted.
I got by this far to start over.
New life, new job, new friends, new lover.
Once upon a time I thought I was gonna go insane.
A couple of years later I'm still here
So bring the pain.
I had to get out of my old town.
I hit the freeway and just drove as fast as I could south bound.
I had to change my religion.
I had to look for life in another galaxy.
I had to change my vision.
Sometimes I let my anger and my past get the best of me.
I let down my guard and get consumed
By all that is negative energy.
I hate when I let myself fall that far back.
Dear God, help me find the energy,
Help me find the willpower that I lack.

Dear God, I'm trying to change,
I'm trying not to be the same.
I walk around with these broken shackles.
I'm ready to start, so bring the pain.
I know I need to forgive and forget.
There is more to life.
I have to let go of all this trauma I carry and let go of regret.
The fire is starting to burn strong in my soul.
I fall to my knees and pray, Father please let me let go.
Its time to dispose of this nagging burden.
I've got the best gift nobody can take away,
That's my children.
They will help me recover and regroup.
Ive got my foundation.
Lets put up these four walls and put up my new roof.
I'm patient and faithful in my Lord
That in time He will help me regain.
I'm sure I'm standing here for a reason.
Im ready to begin.
I'm ready...so bring the pain.

I Will

You always say why I don't say, "I love you," enough.
Well you're right.
I have to stop saying that.
It's because my last two years have been so tough.
The truth is I have to start giving us a chance.
My dark clouds are parting and the light has
Shined down on this romance.
Hun, look at me, put your face in my hands.
You're giving me everything,
Now I need to make you understand.
This has been a long time coming.
I've spent my last seventeen years with the wrong person.
When it was you I should've been loving.
I want to open my door, baby its all you.
You're the only one I owe, *mi amor*.
There is nothing I cant do.
I would swim to the ends of the earth for you.
Hun, I know I've stumbled and fell a few times.
But this is our first day of forever.
This next lifetime is yours and mine.

There is no worry, let me kiss the back of your neck
And whisper in your ear.
Hun let go of all your insecurities;
Our future is here.
And I have to admit,
That when your with me my heart stands still.
Honey, for you I will.
And if I have to admit that when we touch I feel fulfilled.
Baby I will…
And if I have to admit that with you I can just chill.
My love I will.
And if I have to admit that the rest of my life
I want to spend it with you.
My sweetness, I do.
And when you search my heart and search my memory,
Nothing but notes and pictures overflowing
With visions of Valerie.

Tu Carino

You brought me into this world,
When they made you they broke the mold.
You were there everytime I fell and scraped my knee.
You taught me about life.
You helped me to see.
You were there like no other.
You taught me about hard work when
It should've been my father.
I seen you fall, I seen you cry.
No matter how many times were you always managed to smile,
You would always try.
When I was a teen and pushed away,
You always pushed back.
You brought common sense when all I ever did was lack.
You helped bring reality when I dropped out of school.
You helped me to realize that my mind and my two hands
Are my strongest tool.
You were quick to open your doors.
You were the first to offer open arms
When I went through my painful divorce.

When the whole world turned their back on me
Without a care.
All you ever did was give.
I don't think I could ever do what you did,
No matter how long I will live.
Even in your current age,
You continue you continue to pray for me just to make sure
I stay out of danger.
I know I'm really gonna hurt
When the Lord comes calling for an extra angel.
Despite all this I will admire tu carino.
I will always be your baby boy.
I will always be your nino.

" "

Here it is in front of me a blank page.
I look back at my life with players and actors like one grand stage.
I see many scenes acted out.
Some happy, some sad, some filled with rage
Toward people I called friends, family, people I trusted.
Thought I lost it.
Now my pen is my weapon of choice.
The blinders are off so is the gag, I now have a voice.
The pen is my sword, sharp like a knife.
I will cut you and slice you with every written word.
I know a person who thought she had the last laugh.
I may have gone down but I moved on
When the day came and I tore your picture in half.
Through all this, I will rise.
Through all the hypocrisy,
Through all the hate, all the lies,
When you read this can you relate?
Are you in a relationship when all you ever did was give.
And now it's a little too late?
Do you feel like you've lost all hope?
I know how you feel like your at the end of your rope.

Pick yourself up, believe it or not,
You are a hidden success.
There is a light at the end of your tunnel.
Look beyond your mess.
Believe it or not there is power in prayer.
Let all your troubles give way, let someone else be a hater.
Try this experiment.
I feel your pain , I had your life.
I was living it, as you read this just what do you see?
Close your eyes; do you see yourself?
Or are you just an image of me?
Those empty quotations at the top of this page.
Put in your own title, you are the creator.
The actors, the players,
This time you set the stage!

No Excuses

Carried too much in my heart like a heavy load.
Called it quits with my head down as I hit the road.
All that had happened I blamed on others.
People went on with their lives.
I could die tomorrow and nobody would've bothered.
That was then but this now.
I still have my days,
But today I've let go of the frown.
I've put my past behind me
And gave my middle finger to the world.
I'm worth more than that
And my plans are filled with gold.
Ive got great friends who give me great advice.
And I hang on their every word.
Day by day my painful past a little blurred.
I wish that person who had hurt me all the very best.
I still wake every morning and thank God
So I'm assured I can pass every test.
Don't get into a battle of words
Because the first who speaks only loses.
Im glad she's found happiness without me,
So I have no excuses.

Got the good Lord more in my life
And all I can do is pray and listen.
I'm still not perfect but I've finally found
What I've been missing.
Ive got air in my lungs, God in my heart,
And freedom on my mind.
My goal is to stop blaming someone else
And to concentrate on happiness I will soon find.
I know life goes on, even though I'm not fully healed
From my broken heart, scrapes and bruieses.
But everyday I climb that hill
And get that much closer to the top.
Theres no more excuses.

Craving On You

Hey hun just writing this to say
Just how much I enjoy your company.
Just how you make my day.
How I get an urge to see you when I'm alone,
And just not enough to hear
Your sexy voice over the phone.
That way you walk around the bedroom
In those tiny tight biker shorts.
Its so wicked what you wear.
No matter what Im doing I freeze and I have to stare.
I have to say come over and give me some sugar,
Momma come bring your delicious body over here
And give me somma.
All kinds of love and attention.
I get an unquenchable thirst for your undying affection.
Anything from simple jeans to that black sexy halter
Theres something about you that sends my heart into a flutter.
Love running my fingers up and down your thighs.
You should be an illegal drug cause you make me so high.
And what is about those deep dimples on each side of your cheek.
Im such a lucky man I got what I always wanted.
I no longer do I have to seek.

You touch me in areas where I just melt.
You touch on nerves I never even knew I had.
Ive never even felt..
There's a million reasons why but this note only has a few
Let's lock the door behind us so I can show
Why you've got me craving on you.

Santa Monica

Oh Santa Monica,
Where have you been all my life?
Why is it when I'm here
Everything seems so right?
I know I can leave my old town behind.
I cant wait to head south
On the 405 and unwind.
Hot air in my face
Then all of a sudden,
I smell the salt water
And I know this is the place.
Its where memories are made
And where dreams broken.
Its in the streets enjoying the sights
With my kids laughing and joking.
Oh Santa Monica.
Where have you been?
I wanna jump on a yacht
Wnd ride the ocean.
I want to be like a kid
And run to the end of the pier.

I want to ride the roller coaster at Pacific Park
Without any fear.
I want to watch the sun set on the beach.
I want time to reflect and think about freedom
And how its all within reach.
If I were rich
This is where I would want to live.
The different smells of food fill the air.
There is so much to see.
Santa Monica has got so much to give.
I want to hold hands with the one I love,
As we watch the street performers on 3rd street promenade.
I want to watch sports
And sit at the bar
As I have some beers at Yankee Doodle
Or have a burger with my kids
At Johnny Rockets
As I watch the rich folks walk their fancy poodles.
All the shopping and the fashion,
At night it becomes a whole different place
You cant even imagine.
If you're single then around the corner
There is a singles club
If you just want to hang with the boys
Theres a tavern, there's a bar, theres a pub.

In the middle of the night
She becomes so serene.
It gets a little colder,
But she becomes a whole different scene.
The Promenade looks like Christmas
With all the lights.
The pier glistens and sparkles
With people laughing.
And having fun all into the night.
In the morning its off to
Maria Sol at the end of the pier
For a good old fashioned Mexican breakfast,
Then afterwards rent a bike
And ride off next door over to Venice.
Watch the tattoo artists
Or the muscle heads,
Watch as the bums get up
And leave to another location
As they fold up their cardboard beds.
Its almost time to say goodbye all too soon.
We take off and pack all our stuff and new treasures.
As we give back our room.
I get back on the 10 east.
There's never a dull moment
Nothing I didn't enjoy the least.

All except everytime I have to say
Goodbye to my old friend.
Santa Monica, I know there will be many.
I find a song I like on the radio and turn it up.
This ones to you.
I'm sure we'll meet again.

Far Gone

Lets you and I be far gone, lets ditch this town lets go on the run.
Lets throw a dart at the map, drive off into the sunset.
With my hand on your lap.
Far gone into the wind, lets not tell anyone
Not even our next of kin.
Lets fill the old gas tank with gas, put on your shades baby
Let's get out here fast..
Turn up the radio, listen to whats on.
Put your hand out the window and just kiss the sun.
Make no plans no reservations, drive into any hotel.
Let there be no hesitation.
Far gone, leave all our worries and our stress, lets hit the beach.
Lets hit the club, hit the bed, get into each others heart
Into each other's soul into each others head.
Run out onto the shore, run out onto the pier.
Lets watch the sunset lets share a beer,
And share each others love ininterrupted.
Far gone , lets drive all along the coast, take plenty of pictures.
Buy a bottle of wine and give each other a toast.
Lets bring on the night lets anticipate,
Lets jump into the Jacuzzi lets celebrate.

Its not too often we leave everything far behind.
Its not too often we go with our hearts
And forget about our mind.
On the way home lets laugh
And recall everything we just did.
You sing a song and i'll just hum.
Back to being normal and crazy
And now far gone.

Rumble In My Heart

Nobody tries to fail, but most fail to try.
These words have so much meaning
Fom the darkest moments when I just wanted to die.
Leave the whole world behind
Because I didn't want to suffer.
I just wanted to experience life in the hear after.
I didn't see how fast I had fallen
I thought I was left behind one of the forgotten.
I would wake up crying, and after I'd get home
Id go to sleep just thinking about dying.
I'd pop pills just to try and end it all.
I broke down doors, tried to hurt others
Only to be stopped by the law.
I wanted to just disappear like the wind.
I grew tired of trying to be happy
So tired of trying to pretend.
I constantly cried out like I was a victim.
Constantly blamed others and pointed the finger at the system.
Oh so many bad thoughts just moved in heavy rotation.
I was going berserk, paranoia messing with my imagination.
But eventually time does heal all wounds.
I lifted myself out like battered soldier out of a platoon.

There was a loud crash and thunder

That brought me to a halt.

I analyzed myself from afar after

And realized everything was really only my fault.

Oh Lord help me.

Oh the good Lord had come.

Please forgive me.

Have mercy on me for what I had done.

Please point me in the right direction.

Point me toward the river.

Ask whatever you want my Father

And I shall deliver.

I will forever have faith

From here on out to my dying days.

I have opened myself to you as my savior.

Its never too late for a fresh start.

I have cried out to you with a rumble in my heart.

Eternal

I want to be out in an open field,
Want to visit the church where I first kneeled.
Want to be left alone with my bible,
Want to look up into the heavens and smile.
Want to feel the Lord's embrace.
I close my eyes and feel the sunshine
Touch down upon my face.
I want to be one with the Lord.
I want to walk in his eternal garden
When I leave this world.
I look back at everything I ever did wrong.
I look back at the times I was confused like I didn't belong.
So many things that were once a blur are now so clear.
I look at life now with a better perspective
And a little more patience.
I trust in the Lord.
He has me in his care no matter what the situation I am in.
Everything that is good shall prevail.
Our lord is about chances.
No matter how many times we fail.
I don't fear the unexpected.
I don't fear the unknown.

No matter whatever happens I know I am never alone.
So much time to live and so little time to forgive.
I want to open my heart and set my mind free.
I want to let go of bitterness and animosity.
I just want to turn the page and follow His every word.
I look forward to the day I am eternal
And forgiven as I serve my Lord.

McFarland

I remember walking the streets of McFarland.
Just a little boy but so bad wanting to be a man.
Right there on California avenue.
Our two story home, but we only rented the top floor.
Right after school, we'd be there all day.
Cause mom and dad worked but grandpa lived next door.
Soon as they'd arrive, we couldn't wait
My brothers and I would run.
Or on our bikes sometimes even skates.
We would go meet up with our cousins
Who lived over on the corner of California and Sherwood.
Off to the park or even Mouser field
We were crazy kids always up to no good.
Raul, Rachel and Carmen,
We'd stay out late
But time seemed so much slow back then.
I drive by today on my way to work and think
Like I used to walk that bridge just a short fat kid.
My brothers and I would attend St. Elizabeth for Catechism.
Times we were so innocent then man I miss them.
Boy all them streets , Perkins, San Lucas.

Went to school down Kern Avenue.
Still seems like the same old
Little town nothing new.
My bud Ruben lives there,
My brother for life Robert and his wife Maggie.
He's raising his family on the east side.
It may not seem like a lot to some people
But I will always have a spot for that place
And it still makes me feel right.
Nothing but great memories as a kid.
But today I am a man.
Nevertheless the flashbacks start flooding my head
When I pass by McFarland.

2nd Time Around

You're probably contemplating right now all by yourself
What is there to do when all else fails?
Thought I left all these feelings in my past,
But seems like de'javu is gaining on me fast.
It seemed like no miracle would help,
You wouldn't budge and didn't care how I felt.
It seemed like it could've been just another day.
It wasn't enough that I convinced you to stay.
Shit just kept getting loud,
You'd think we could've learned from our 2nd time around.
Don't you wish we could press a button
To put everything in reverse?
Don't you wish this was some movie set
Snd we had a chance to rehearse?
Time and time again we got too much of the same.
Tired of playing goodguy
And getting fed the same dish of fucking lame.
Look girl, I would take you back in an instance.
I would wish you would cooperate and face less resistance.
I wont lie that I go to sleep easy at night,
But its sometimes nice to go just a day without a fight.

Seems like yesterday when we tied the knot.

I didn't care that July was hot.

You looked like a princess in your dress

And me in my tux.

Fast forward to the present

We're both sleeping in separate roofs

And this relationship just sucks.

And sometimes I don't know whether to laugh or cry.

I keep hoping for a miracle.

Don't really want to cut all ties.

But I feel like I'm lost at sea and im about to drown

This could've been avoided.

You and I could've been better

Our 2nd time around.

40

I am not afraid of dying, not afraid of death.
I'm more concerned where I'll be when I take my last breath.
Don't fear much these days.
My strangest fear has always been my age.
Where am I going?
Don't know where I been.
Feel like Ive taken every hit, taken every blow.
Later this year I'll be turning 40,
Feel sad like im turning old too quick in a hurry.
Now days I take it with a grain of salt.
Don't regret much anymore,
Because half of all my bad moments from my past
Were partially all my fault.
Learned to love life, got me a good woman, found God.
When I do die I hope I am surrounded by my family.
Because Lord knows this life wasn't much good to me.
Sometimes I just hate the person looking at me.
That boy looked much better when he was just 33.
What's with all these crow feet around my eyes?
And this little belly that just wont go away?
My knees hurt and its getting harder to get out of bed everyday.

Feel like a weathered rockstar with so many stories
From his days on the road.
My God, I just hate getting old.
But on the flip side I've got no more skeletons.
Nothing to hide.
I'm discovering a new wealth of wisdom.
I've let God into my life
And I'm enjoying this new freedom.
Ive let him lay out the plans he's got set for me.
Ive learned to live one day at a time.
No room for misery.
Where I go from here its truly unknown.
Like a butterfly hatching from its cocoon,
My true colors have finally shown.

Boy Becomes The Man

What became of the boy
Looking through his telescope up at the stars?
Playing city in his room
With his hot wheels cars.
Punishing himself in a corner,
Whenever he got into trouble?
Never had plenty of friends,
Usually a loner.
Coffee table, always finding an answer
For everything cause he was curious and able.
Watching his Disney VHS tapes
And his love for Barney.
Always happy with smiles and thinking corny.
Generous, kind, and independent,
Quick to fight for his beliefs and quick to defend it.
What became of the boy
Looking too frail for his first wrestling practice?
Collecting Pokemon cards?
Harry Potter books and losing his Gameboy game cartridges?
Often misunderstood?
Quite often looked down upon
By so called family members as no good?

What became of the boy fighting through his confusion
Of life and his own personal hell?
Quite often blaming everything negative on only himself?
Often put on the sidelines
And never complaining or saying a word.
He turned his life around when he became reborn
And rededicated his life to the Lord.
My son may the sun always shine on your face.
And the wind always at your back.
Always live for the present
But never become to big that you forget your past.
As you carve out your own niche in life
As you finally discover where you stand.
What became of that boy?
Well he finally became the man.

The Hurt

I know it was only 4 years.
But I felt like I had known you all my life.
We shared so many happiness and tears.
I live every waking minute haunted.
Wishing I could take back.
I can almost see you in someone elses arms right now.
Probably happy, living your dream, probably settled down.
Wish I could've given you what you wanted.
Seems like everything I did I would only fail.
No matter what, I wish you the best.
Whatever new wind has caught your sail.
The heart forgives what the mind doesn't forget.
I don't want to bash you and recall the bad moments.
I know, meeting you, I will never regret.
Wish I had something more of you.
But all I have are these tears.
That's all I got out of this relationship,
Those are my souveniers.
I've gone back, erased all our pictures from my Facebook page.
It hurts so much to see your beautiful face.
It's the only way to move myself forward onto the next stage.

I always thought we'd grow old together.

We had some beautiful moments.

Now you're someone elses forever.

I've hit rock bottom before.

Not my first time falling down in the dirt.

Not my first time had my heart broken.

But you just never get over the hurt.

Mother

Oh my mother, the sadness she has seen.
But always to me is the happiness she brings.
Oh my mother, as far as I can remember,
You have always been.
We've had our differences and fights.
But through it all I knew until the end
You were always right.
Oh my mother, you are all sacrifice
Through all the hurt and all the pain,
You've always been honest,
You tell me no lies.
What you see is what you get.
I truly love you.
You may forgive but you never forget.
Oh my mother, your love is as deep as the river runs.
And as genuine as the morning sun.
A beautiful angel with a heart of gold.
You live not just in my life.
But a part of forever, a part of my world.

Dreams

I dream away, away away
To another world, another life another day.
The minute I sleep, my ear buds onto my ears,
I drift away and forget my troubles,
Forget my worries, forget my fears.
I get lost in song, get hung on every note, every word.
I'm not weak, I become brave, I am strong.
Where dreams may go or dreams may come.
They might translate or mean something to some.
I love the feeling of drift and release.
In my dreams I don't feel my feet but I fall to my knees.
My life is played out like some music video
With music in the back and shot in black and white.
People I know, places I been, things I've seen,
It all comes to me without delay
The minute I put the ear buds on my ears
I close my eyes....
I dream away...away...away.

Bro

The word bro is thrown around pretty loosely.
Im not making a huge deal
But in this case it happened to me.
Take for instance my "bro" Bob.
We had so much in common,
Like doing our wives crooked
To having the same line of job.
Fast forward to the present,
God rewarded him with greatness.
Meanwhile I started on my descent.
Very hard I would plummet and fall.
I make no excuses it was all my fault,
Destined to lose it all.
But through it, you remained an angel.
You were there for me with good advice,
You always kept me out of danger.
Throughout the years
You never changed your mood.
No matter what success you remained genuine.
A stand up guy, great attitude.
You were like a true brother.

I felt like I known you all my life,
Like as if we were from the same mother.
Yes sometimes your words were a bit harsh.
You showed me tough love
And you made sense
When push came to shove.
But it seemed like the tougher it took me
To get off my feet,
You started to treat me like a loser.
Like I was beneath.
Like I was like some of your other friends.
Who your wife didn't like.
Because they didn't fit your new lifestyle.
I could feel the pressure,
I could feel the heat.
I wasn't in denial.
Brother, I loved your kids like if they were my own.
I had the upmost respect for your wife.
I helped you move into your new massive home.
Yeah, it hurt when you let me move in with you.
For those four weeks
You made me feel like shit.
You treated me like dirt.
I know I hurt and treated people wrong.
But you were my brother.

God strike me down
If I ever betrayed your trust.
I dare you name one!
You took advantage
Cause you saw me battered and bruised.
But brother, you couldn't be further from the truth.
So maybe I never made the right descisions,
But you knew me from day one
I always followed my own intuitions.
Homie, you decided to dissolve our friendship
Cause you couldn't stand my wife?
Brother I would never let any harm
Come over my children.
I just wanted to be happy and start a new life.
I thought you would be happy.
Thought you would be proud.
But instead of walking into direct sunlight,
My world was greeted with a dark cloud.
Ten years, brother all the talk,
All the family moments.
The changes, the tears.
Bro have you got no balls?
God forbid you ever walk into my shoes.
Cause then and only then
You'll see where the chips fall.

Oh and lets not even bring religion.
Cause we know you're too good for that too.
You could care less to listen.
Bro you were my homie,
You were like my blood.
Next time you call someone, "bro,"
Think about it and shut the fuck up.

Sick And Tired Of Being Sick And Tired

Been wanting to write lately but I have no inspiration.
Just been bogged down with excess sadness and frustration.
Seems like the more I try the further back I get in life
Makes me so angry, just makes me want to cry.
Its the same routine, everythings the same.
Same old shit I've already seen.
Get out of bed for my measly dime.
My bones crack, my feet hurt.
Im battered and bruised but always get up on time.
Hit the shower, as I brush my teeth.
As I catch a glimpse of the guy in the mirror, my day goes sour..
So tired of the daily grind working for nothing.
Breaking my back and losing my mind.
I fear I will get old so soon that my kids will forget me.
Don't want to end up like my dad in the hospital
Sitting there so lonely.
Dear God, if you could take me now I wish you could.
I make nobody happy, Im going nowhere.
I'm useless, I'm no good.
I don't want to take my own life.
Cause I would feel like a cheat.

I guess I have some sort o f dignity or pride
Cause I cant admit defeat.
Get home and fight with the wife.
I aint got my kids.
My world feels so cold and dark
Why even have a life?
Sucks to always be broke.
Feel like a broken record,
Pretend to be happy.
But deep down I am just a joke.
Nobody understands,
So Im tired of talking.
I see people I cant stand on a daily basis.
So tired of the tension
even sicker of the phony faces.
I plead with you God.
If you do listen,
What is my purpose here?
Take me home,
Light up my ignition.

If I Could

If I could I would rock you in my arms
And force you never to grow.
It hurts to see your Facebook pictures
And not recognize my little girl.
If I could I would've read to you that bedtime story
Just a little bit longer
Didn't ever see it then
But I see it now
The pains of a father.
If I could I would've stopped the hands of time then
To see you born, walk and grow all over again.
If I could I would turn back time,
Back to where you were 5, 7, or 8
And right before you hit your teens
Turn it back quick before its too late.
If I could I would freeze your first dance recital,
Look at my baby tippy toes across the stage
A tear rolls down because you inspire.
If I could I would erase this pain of growing older
And seeing you less, I feel like your forgetting me,
This I hate to confess.

I wish you could look like the baby pics
That adorn my walls.
With every year another wrinkle another teardrop falls.
Someday when I'm gone
and I happen to waltz across your mind.
Don't think of me as the sad old man.
But the young happy father I was.
Then hit rewind.
Still not used to you having so many plans.
I guess it's selfish to think you'd have time to call
Or write your old man.
Sorry that your mom and I couldn't make it work.
Wish I could've been the dad
I really wanted to become sometimes
And not the bitter old jerk.

Honey

Hey honey, hey my love.
You make me feel strong you make me grow weak.
You still make me melt when you smile
And I see your dimples on each side of your cheek.
Hey love, hey honeybunches.
You make me feel like the man I want to be
With your magical touches.
Hey pookie, hey gorgeous.
Yes you're sexy, you're my dream woman.
You're what every woman should be.
Sorry never finished this.
Cause the bitch quit on me.

4 ½ Years

What are we doing here?
After all the fighting, all the arguments, all the tears.
It has finally come to this,
We're about to go our separate ways.
Back to being strangers, not even one last kiss.
We could've worked this out so easily,
We could've found some middle ground
Instead of sleeping with the enemy.
But I guess it was only inevitable.
Call me foolish, call me crazy, even gullible.
We both knew it was gonna end.
We were both tired of the games, so tired of playing pretend.
One thing for sure, I still love you.
But I guess this separation is the best cure.
Who would've thought our last date,
The day after Valentines,
Who would've thought
That time we'd see each other for the last time.
That was one rare moment,
Where we were happy, do you remember?

But I just couldn't love you
And ignore the other people in my life.
Loving you cut both ways like a dull knife.
But I do hope you find that special someone
That you wanted me to be,
Since all I ever brought you was burden,
Sadness, and misery.
Just remember I texted you at work
Wanting to still work this out,
But you were dead set.
You were already clouded with heavy doubt.
You said our marriage had "run its course."
But I felt we still could've saved it
Cause we had seen worse.
I wish you hadn't let me pack and walk.
God knows I tried but you still didn't give a fuck.
But I know you'll never quit.
I wish you happiness and you find Mr. perfect.
As for me im in no rush for somebody else.
Too afraid to fall in love again
Only to see it fail.
I've lost you for good this time
But we'll always have the memories.
Guess we're better apart
Than living like sworn enemies.

God bless you and may life be good to you,
It was only four and a half years,
But there were wonderful moments in there too.

Bad EX'perience

Feel like I just stepped out of a long stay in prison.
Should be happy but I cant help feeling
Like there is something missing.
For a minute I thought I had it all.
Kinda felt it coming
But I still couldn't prevent myself for the fall.
In the end envy was all you got.
You were the love for me I always dreamed of,
But in the end I guess you were not.
Just sucks cause you cant fight the feelings.
Sucks even more thinking of the time it will take
To erase this bad experience.
Nothing can be further from the truth.
You make me out to be the monster,
When in the end I was the one left battered and bruised.
Well your mom finally got her wish.
she never liked me anyway
Cause I was poor and never showed
Any signs of ever striking it rich.
Now she can finally make you like her.
A lonely drunk after all she's likely bound for the floor.

So tired of fighting anyway to prove myself.
Never got any further but constant hell.
That's cool though.
I'll rebuild the bridges I've burned.
You've held me back enough now its my turn.
You've always wanted to erase
The excess baggage I brought into your life.
You knew what I came with from the beginning.
You were more of a tyrant than a wife.
Cant believe you teach Christianity what a joke.
If people only knew the real you,
You'd be out of work.
Somedays thought I found myself hurting for you.
Your love and the feel of a woman.
What could've been or a good blessing.
Turned out to be a bad omen.
I got to pick myself up,
And harden my heart.
Time for another fresh start.
This is just another test to my resilience.
Live and learn from my bad experience.

Till We Meet Again

Cant believe I let you slip through my fingers again.
Could've sworn it was real or was I just dreaming?
I just cant comprehend.
Seemed like only yesterday.
I messed up on the woman I married, for you?
I never got over you.
We did have crazy times that to this day
Still make me chuckle in silent dismay.
We've crossed each other's paths since then.
I must admit I always missed you my old friend.
Only now the roles are reversed.
You've got your husband and family,
And I'm going through my second divorce.
Couldn't believe the elation in my heart
When I saw your number on my screen.
My head spun to yesterday
and it was like the old days it seems.
Too good to be true I guess,
But I'm glad it didn't go any further.
Wouldn't want to put your family through this mess.

And even though you tell me you're happy in your marriage
I'm glad you're trying to work it out.
You've got so much going on.
Stay positive, don't let there be any doubt.
We'll always have the past.
I remember watching you smile and laugh
As you sat on my passenger side as I drove fast.
To your house, to the park, every song, every lyric.
Has left a memory;
A permanent mark.
I have always dreamed someday you'd be mine.
Maybe not now, maybe not next year
Maybe there will be another time.
I see you have unfriended me on Facebook.
I don't blame you, had to do what was right.
At least I got to see what your new life was like.
At least I got one last look.
You know I will always have a spot in my heart
for you my dear friend.
Maybe not now, maybe another lifetime,
Til we meet again.

Fucking Hate That I Still Fucking Love You

This house is lonely and quiet.
Thought I'd be over you by now
But unfortunately not yet.
I can still feel you, almost seen your ghost.
Miss your laughter, your beauty, your scent the most.
I stare at these same four walls.
Stare at the flowers I gave you for Valentines
As the last petal falls.
I stand in the kitchen
Where we had our last big fight.
I still sleep in the room
Where we last made love for that final night.
I can still hear your laughter
I can almost see you greeting me
As you fall into my embrace.
Your illusion goes straight through me
And I'm back in my lonely place.
Why did it end?
Have you no remorse?
We always promised we'd stick together.
We never spoke a word of divorce.

I wonder who's loving you now?
I try to be happy but I cant help but feel so down.
We've both invested so much.
I should be happy but damn,
I miss your touch.
Why didn't you try harder
Why did you quit?
Girl you always knew I had kids from a previous,
So don't give me that shit.
I hated how we were always on a different page.
I honestly did love you.
But your insecurities always flew me into a rage.
Its not fair cause I didn't want this.
But I couldn't betray my kids,
But why are there still things that I feel that I miss?
Here I sit drinking the last of my brew.
I can get over this
But I still fucking hate that I still fucking love you.

I Am What I Am

I am what I am.
A child of God, just a regular man.
I've made plenty of mistakes
Too many to count.
I used to think being angry was the best way to go.
I admit I was lost now I am found.
Broke some hearts had mine broken too
In return lost a true love,
Re-married to the wrong one,
Live and learn.
Burned lots of bridges,
Slept with plenty of bitches.
Never afraid to be single.
Just hate to work so hard for someone
Only to be blamed with an accusing finger.
I have plenty of haters all for no reason.
Some friends, some family.
No matter how hard you try
Theres never any pleasing.
I keep a tight circle of friends
And nothing else matters.

Top of my list are my kids.

And mom and knowing that kinda love never shatters.

I know I'm not squeaky clean.

I've been unfaithful, irresponsible, grudgeful,

And plain mean.

But at least I've mattered enough to own up to it.

I love to work hard

Finish what I begin and never quit.

I'm a fun loving, good hearted soul.

I believe everyone deserves a second chance.

My worst enemies and my many foes.

Good people are always high in demand.

I'm not one of them cause I'm not perfect.

But I am what I am.

Hellish Life

My hellish life is all I ever seen.
Crazy people, crazy shit,
Crazy places in my mind I've been.
Oh to be young again,
Seems like nothing bad ever happened
Things were so innocent back then.
And if you say there he goes singing the blues,
I'd say don't judge til you've walked a mile in my shoes.
You know what fuck them
But then fuck them too!
Cause I married the wrong people who broke my heart,
Heaven knows I fought and tried
And loyal til the day we would part.
Yeah, I know I was never an angel.
I did stupid stuff
I walked by the face of danger.
After all the crazy drama I seen,
I can honestly say
Im still a pretty honest human being.
Must have all started with my father,
The way I was raised
And later the way he wronged my daughter.

This hellish life that I have lead,

The ghosts and demons still lurk around in my head.

Despite all that I have done wrong

I have a good support system

In my homies and my bro's.

We throw back a few

As we listen to some Vicente songs.

I'm a better man cause everything I been through.

I still have my critics who love to remind me of my past.

I ignore them cause I know

They have nothing better to do.

Tired of living this life of being the same

Tired of getting hurt and going insane.

Tired of being lonely and why this shit only happens to me.

I'm getting stronger better and a yearning to be free.

Cause I carry the scars

From being burned down to the bones.

But at the end I'll leave you amazed

At how this Phoenix has rose.

Rewind

Haven't slept a wink.
All I do is put everything in rewind
And it makes me think.
Lost so much sleep,
Lost so much weight
Cause I cant eat.
I put everything into perspective,
And I cant understand
How your memory is so selective.
You tell people I never did anything for you?
You tell people I was a monster.
You tell people I was loveless and cruel.
But everyone knows well.
I worked my fingers to the bone to make you happy
And all you ever returned was just hell.
I took you places I couldn't even afford,
Yet you still whined how you were constantly ignored.
But I did it to retaliate
The way you treated me
And how you would always humiliate.

You were hurtful to my kids from a previous.
You treated them like strangers
And always acted so jealous and devious.
Rewind to that final week.
We were like total strangers
We didn't even speak.
We hardly even touched.
We both saw the writing on the wall
And nothing meant much.
I hardly even slept.
I would lay staring at the ceiling as you wept.
I could feel the weight of your stare.
But I wasn't gonna back down.
You brought this on yourself
When you decided to be unfair.
That final day as I loaded up my stuff
It hurt how you failed to compromise,
But what would've been the use
After a while I got used to see through your lies.
Just how can I get away from your kind.
Tear off my rear view mirror.
Put this truck in fast forward,
And never again put anything in rewind.

Unapologetic

Unapologetic about the way I feel.
Why should I apologize?
Not being fake is who I am.
Being me, being for real.
So I burned plenty of bridges.
Broke a few hearts,
But I too left myself with plenty of stitches.
Unapologetic if I can't stay single for long.
But I cant stay locked away in my room writing sad songs.
Left many jobs, posted hurtful stuff about my past.
If you don't want to read it
Quit pretending to care and kiss my ass.
Forgive me if you don't agree with the people I socialize with.
To put it mildly I don't give a shit.
If at the remains of the day, I let people dictate
And do as they say,
I'd be ecstatic on the outside
But inside I'd be filled with sorrow.
I wouldn't be able to gauarantee
I'd still be here tomorrow.

But today here I stand
Laughing with my friends and my girl
And a beer in my hand.
Unapologetic about my dark days being far behind.
Ive finally put my life in order,
I'm happy I'm feeling fine.
Found someone who isn't a risk.
Someone who actually cares and loves my kids.
Unapologetic for finding again a new beginning.
I'm crazy, feeling inspired, dancing and singing.
Once upon a time, I was so down under
Now look at me rock and roaring like thunder.
From the ashes the old Phoenix has risen.
Unapologetic how I feel today
Could care less if you refuse to listen.

Gone 4 Good

From the minute I unpacked in my new place.
I was sad for a minute
But slowly a smile has crawled back onto my face.
You see I'm glad your finally gone for good.
You always held me down
And your attitude always spoiled my mood.
Im glad to say I wasn't the one who quit.
I put up with your extreme jealousy and your psycho shit.
I was a loyal husband and still you drove me down
And you still couldn't trust me
since the day I slipped on that band.
So now me on my own.
I'm doing what I wanna do
And being bad to the bone.
I see the fog has started to lift.
I finally realized my true talents,
My dreams, and I know I have a gift.
So who cares what crap you have to say.
This is the 3rd time we split.
Your own fault you let me get away.

I still keep a prayer in my heart,
But I think the best remedy for our ill marriage
Was to just part.
There is so much I always wanted to do,
Now I can cause the biggest obstacle I had in my life
Was you!
You're gone for good, you're gone for good,
You're gone for good, Ive been a nice guy for too long.
Now it feels kinda right to sound fucking rude.
Feels so so good to feel the shine of the sun.
Ive walked out of the darkness
Feel so free.
I can have my heart on a special someone.
Im not trying to be arrogant
Cause if you know me you would know
I did the best I could.
But you can only get kicked so much.
Thank God almighty you're gone for good.

The Writer

Here sits the lonely writer pen in hand,
Trying to make sense out of life
Trying to understand.
Blank paper in front of my face
I close my eyes and think back to a different time
a different place.
I seem to have better material
When I'm depressed or angry.
Sometimes I write better when im isolated and lonely.
My bitch wife once asked me
Why I don't write happy stuff about our marriage.
Couldn't make miracles happen
It would be a miscarriage.
But just piss me off and you my friend
Might find yourself in a rhyme.
Out of my poison pen
And straight out of my twisted mind.
My life is an open book.
I'm not ashamed.
Love me or hate me but you cant resist but to take a look.

But I cant write at a drop of a dime.

I need peace,

I need to bare out my inner feelings.

I need time.

So I daydream of what it would be able to appear.

Walking alone

Arms stretched out in an open field.

Gazing up at the sky, wondering what my future holds.

Not even fearing the day I die.

Thinking back at the hearts Ive broken,

My past struggles,

My sadness, and all the bridges left

Still smoldering and smoking.

I know life is a journey.

Our map is our bible and our leader is God.

I fall, I crawl, I stumble,

But always get up.

Always looking inspired to write.

Pacing, listening to music, frustrated, but not tonight.

Here sits the writer pen in hand.

No Fame

What if we were born with no name?
Would all my troubles, all my burdens.
All my sadness, remain the same?
Last night I was lost in thought,
Looking back at the bridges I burned
And the battles I fought.
I've survived, scarred and broken,
The people I have always loved
I've kept close to my heart
The ones who've drifted I have yet to have spoken.
I've shown no shame, all for survival.
All to love, just to move on, don't need the fame.
Will never give up on the ones I love deep in my soul.
And even after I leave this world
They will feel my presence in my afterglow.
Sometimes I miss the feeling of tranquil.
Most times, my life moves too fast
And I crave the moment to be still.
The beast within is getting harder to tame.
But I could without the drama, without the fame.

Other times I sense the voice of angels.
I feel the warmth within my soul
And I no longer fear danger.
At one time all I wanted was all the glory.
Today I fear the ones I love
Will someday not even know me.
Too much stress, tiring of the sacrifices
And anguish of another test.
Maybe I should take up smoking cigarettes.
My hate right now is in recession.
I despise passing by that town.
I'm plagued by demons I'd rather forget.
I would immediately give up that crazy game.
To forget the battle, to let go of the resentments.
Don't need no fame.

Dark Times

Someone once said,
"These are dark times indeed."
I don't know,
He must've known what he was talking about
Or maybe he was just high on weed.
I grip the steering wheel tight
And just keep on driving.
Forget there was one cop car
Now I hear an army of sirens.
Maybe three or four
Or maybe a dozen.
Despite their orders for me to pull over
The whole scene seems like everything is on mute
Cause I do nothing.
This will be my blaze of glory.
Somebody somewhere will remember me,
Remember this day,
Remember this crazy story.
Despite all the commotion,
My entire body and mind
Is consumed by enraged emotion.

Black and white flashbacks
Race through my mind.
Memories of the birth of all three of my kids
Everything spins into rewind.
The father I could've been.
The end of my marriage,
All the hardship I have seen.
Cars race out of my way on the busy street.
I look up at my rear.
Cant believe I will end this way.
I think oh well this old dog seen.
Sick of my life anyways tired of all the shit.
This has really got to happen,
Just like Michael Jackson's this is it.
Turn up the radio, hear a song by Adelle.
She always makes me feel better
Whenever I fail.
I feel good at least for my girls.
They will be taken care of.
Their mothers married Mr. Perfect.
My son is a better man.
I'm just another reject.
Who's gonna miss me?
I caused a lot of pain in my life.
Made myself a lot of misery.

Like an old song says,
"Funny when you die how people start listening."
Im almost on the freeway,
I'm almost out of time.
Twisted long faces, all crying people
Who came around from different places.
Yeah I could see it now, my own funeral.
I'll be remembered for that day and then forgotten as usual.
Cant believe Im doing this poem right in my head
As all this is going on, cant see myself finishing this.
Cause soon I'll be gone.
Cant finish this last line.
Im blocked and my tires wont move
And now I'm out of time.

Things Left Unsaid

One minute your sitting on my lap and looking into my eyes.
The next minute were kissing each other goodbye.
What a way to end almost four years.
So many misunderstandings,
So much jealousy, so many tears.
Why couldn't you swallow your pride instead?
Could've saved so much heartbereak.
Couldve left on a better note,
Than having left so many things left unsaid.
I miss watching TV with you all alone.
Going out on dates,
Being in bed in our cozy home.
Why did you let your jealous ways destroy us?
Why couldn't you be mature?
Now I look at our empty house.
I cant imagine this loss.
You're almond shaped eyes,
The sweet smell of your skin,
I was honest with you about myself.
We both knew what we had going in.

I hate to see you cry.

I hate to see you turn red.

We had it going for ourselves.

Now we both have gone on

With things left unsaid.

I thank God for the day I met you,

Looked like my personal hell days

were finally through.

I don't want to fall in love again

But I loved your kids.

You were my chosen one.

You were my answer.

You claimed I never loved you

But each day I was falling faster and faster.

I knew this was too good to be true.

You walked out.

I was left holding the bag like a fool.

Never did I imagine this.

Never did I let that thought cross my head.

You want to start over.

We've already lost so much.

And I left so many things left unsaid..

F(aith) You

Just got done listening to the word.
So glad in my life I have the good Lord.
Don't care what news
Comes out of that little bird.
I've seen my destiny.
Could also care less
What you think about me.
Got a stack of bills that are long overdue.
Got stress and worries
Most days I don't know what to do.
But then it comes to me.
I've got the Lord, got a job.
I've really hate people I cant stand,
Wish I could eliminate..
Then it hits me, I've got the lord.
Just got my PG&E turned off and my cable shut off.
It never stops
Just when I think I've had enough.
Hello?...Got the Lord.
Had another fight with the wife.
Her son's annoying me to hell sometimes.
I wish sometimes I wish I could get out of this life.

Then I smile and look up to heaven.
Have the Lord.
People and family still talk trash about me.
At every turn, they can't believe that I've changed.
Get used to it and live and learn.
Now I got the land lord knocking at my door.
They don't believe me
I'm broke this week, gave them what I had.
Every penny, every dollar, not a cent more.
I don't stress, I don't cry, I've got the Lord.
And he knows how hard I try.
Still have the ex.
Still shoveling every penny out of my check.
She don't get that because of her.
My life is still a freaking wreck.
All I can think about is the F word,
But not the offensive one,
The one that makes you believe in the Lord.

2208

It was nothing but a sad lonely shack of a home
Looked so dirty dingy sad and alone.
Nothing but walls and a roof
Grass tall yellow and dried to the roots.
We put all our sweat and tears into it.
It was our dream home for a minute.
Yeah the birth of our youngest daughter
Kids running down the hallway lots of giggles and laughter.
A beautiful windy walkway met up with the front entrance
Right under the front window next to the park bench
My kids little hands decorated the cement..
Many Christmas's and Halloweens,
So much decorating we looked forward to.
It became the home of our dreams.
The kitchen one year became redone.
My wife had a idea and we put it to work
And a patio sprung up to block out the sun.
Our little Chihuahuas made a hole through our screen door
Its funny now, but back then it made us mad
And brought us down.
It was ten years of happiness and bliss.
Some painful moments too I remember and even those I miss.

We knew our neighbors; we knew the whole block,
Hard to believe that dreadful year
When all this would suddenly stop.
I drive by now and then still
And the place looks like a ghost town.
The house seems to look back at me with a sad frown.
I pull over across the street.
I can almost see my kids playing outside.
I could almost see myself mowing the yard
Trying to make it look neat.
We may not live there anymore.
But I'm glad my kids today
Can pull that out from their memory file
And pretend they're still walking into that front door.

Hard To Love

I know I am hard to love.
I know you'll probably like me til you've had enough.
That's cause I constantly have an opinion,
There are no more heroes or fairytales.
Even the good guys wear black and recite wicked spells.
Don't ask me to believe in rainbows and roses;
I am a walking living proof.
I've got the heartache and bruises.
Two wives that can vouch for that I'm hard to love,
Cause I do what I want and give a fuck.
I've got a history of pissing off people here and there
Then I noticed the older I get the less I care.
My best friend once took me in.
But only to berate me about my past.
He tried to make me feel sorry,
Man if I had a nickel for every time..kiss my ass.
He thinks he's the shit he's come so far, which I respect.
But his wife is the man cause she holds his balls in a jar.
I'll do whatever it takes.
I'm not gonna stand to being married
To somebody phony and hang out
With a bunch of fakes..

I'm like a wild flame.
I'm constantly moving
I never stay the same.
I'm hard to love but I been called worse.
I have a dark aura that hangs over me
Like a bad curse.
That's why I'd rather be alone
As long as I have my kids
That's what I call home.
The nicest thing for someone
Was to marry a jealous woman
And be a father to her kids.
Her brother was cool,
Her mother never liked me
And the kid's daddy was a total loser tool.
When I die, I'd rather it be a quick bloody mess.
Don't care for a slow death
Cause my life was everything but blessed.
It's not that I never gave a damn.
It's the people always put so much on me
And in the end I'm just a man.

The Note

Tired of running tired of the fight.
But the further I look the more I see no end in sight.
I've been pulled and stretched in every single direction.
I am stressed beyond the furthest realm
Of the imagination.
There isn't a single day that someone or something
Is breathing down my neck,
And that's no exaggeration.
Hell, there's many things I was looking forward to.
So many things I still wanted to do.
It's tough to look on the bright side
When every waking minute
Your world is black and blue.
Why is my life so screwed up?
Why cant I just get a gun and blow my head off.
Simple I cant afford to get me one.
So much in debt don't have the money to get a gun.
Seems like my bitch ex has gotten away with murder.
She drove me into the ground
And went on with her little life all pretty and in order.
I can almost hear the sirens.
I can almost see the news, watch the headlines.

My life or death was never for me to choose.

So my haters and critics can finally have their day.

They can piss and dance on my grave.

My life has always been a sideshow and a circus.

Outside, I was laughing.

Inside I was dying slow.

So don't cry for me.

Just remember the little good times we had.

Remember for being a friend, a brother

And a good dad..

Don't get me wrong, I do believe in God.

Sometimes I think God just don't believe in me.

Wordz

I'm walking out on an open field.
Somewhere in the middle of nowhere.
Feel numb, cant really say how I feel.
Like I'm in a nightmare, a dream.
Wish I could wake but everything seems so surreal.
Then I touch down to reality,
Hate of not having you next to me.
I somehow had a feeling our time would be limited.
I look back and smile though
Because I'm happy to have experienced it.
For just a minute, for just a second.
For just a blink of an eye everything was fine.
I thought I could've lived with you till the end of time.
You asked for too much and took away from my life
Till I could do no more.
All your insecurities and jealousy
Lead you to walk out that door..
But still I will never hate you.
Even after all the hateful words, I still love you.
I know our life together was just getting harder.
But I know you probably already found another.

Friends say I'm stupid for being too nice.
Maybe because I feel with my heart
And see through the mask and see the lies.
I always gave you the benefit of a doubt.
Even in our darkest moments
When push came to shove
And all we did was fight and shout.
It seemed like we were two tornadoes.
I used to think, "Is it always going to be like this?"
Only heaven knows.
I thank God how we came to this conclusion.
We could've still be living
In some hurtful, romantic illusion.
But today I still think of you and I smile.
Who knows where in this big world you could be?
But I hope wherever you are, you're happy.
And I hope you also think of me
Every once in a while.

I Wish

You're like poison through my blood.
Like cancer in my heart.
Sometimes we get along better when we are further apart.
Just when I think I'm finally over you,
I am haunted by your memories
And nothing could be further from the truth.
Sometimes I wish you could still be curled up in my arms,
Used to love holding you tight
Like I could always keep you from any harm.
I wish I could touch your face and kiss you softly on your cheek.
Miss the magic we used to create between the sheets.
I wish you never would've been so jealous.
We still could've been together right now instead of this big mess.
Wish you never would've walked out.
Honey there was a lot to be worked on,
Lots we could've talked about.
Sometimes I feel like I can still hear your voice.
When I pull up and get home,
The mind can play tricks when your hearts broken
And you're all alone.

This hourglass is gonna be empty soon.
With the last grain of sand.
The light of this relationship is gone
And I'm left a sad lonely man.
Sometimes I wish I could see you just one more time.
Sometimes I wish I could just move on and pretend
Everything is fine.

Chapter 2

Awakenings

This chapter focuses on a relationship I started with a beautiful soul four and a half years later. I learned a lot from her.

Not all is bad here. As a matter of fact this entire chapter is my undying love, appreciation and respect for her, as well as a new found hope she gave me. Her heart is amazing and probably the greatest gifts I took from this relationship were the lessons, the memories, the love, and overcoming awkwardness and jealousy. She taught me to see past that.

Marriage was in the works, but eventually all good things are never meant to last.

So N2U

I wake up thinking of you.
So many happy images of us together
Going through my head just flashing through.
This has been what I always wanted, I needed this.
You're the sunshine in my valley, that heavenly bliss..
I smile when I see your picture on Facebook.
You have a heart of gold
And meeting you was all it took..
For me to fall head over heels
Had to go through so many psycho fakes
To finally fall in love for reals.
Now I'm feeling like a fool,
I'm clumsy, im ditsie, but I'm so into you.
Love sliding my hands around your thighs and hips
I still feel butterflies when my face meets your lips.
And the way you touch me makes me melt
Didn't know this was how real love really felt.
The way you laugh and the glow of your beautiful spirit,
Wish the world would stand still
So I could freeze this minute.
I love how you try to hide

Behind your big sun shades.
I see my inspiration right there
And all my troubles fade.
You turn me on with your shy grin
I don't know how you do it
But you light up my inner erotic sin.
Cant get enough of your hold
Your touch right down to the last kiss
As I drive home cant help but think
You're everything I want
And everything I already miss.
Seems like I was born again and I feel like new.
This only happens when I think, when I feel.
When I love, when I am so so into you.
And I just love watching you undress,
Then when you crawl towards me in bed
There are no worries, there is no stress.
And just the feel of your body
You make me explode I just love
When you play naughty..
If this is what heaven feels like then I guess
I'm already dead,
Cause babe when I'm with you
I never want to leave this California king bed.

And making love to you is only part of the plan.
I want to be wherever you are.
I forever want to be your man.
Making you happy is my number one rule.
Just so happens I love being so into you.

Inspire My Fire

You inspire my fire just when I was about to go nuts.
Losing my faith goes haywire, honey love, sweetie pie.
Baby, hee hee, where were you when I was going crazy?
Its not your fault though
Back then I was trapped in a loveless marriage
Didn't have any idea how my life would go.
Sometimes God puts us with people we think we want
And later when were at the end of our rope
He puts someone else in front.
I remember you from high school,
God I hated those days.
Who would've known years later
My hands would be cradling your lovely face.
God just the way you feel, your scent.
The curves or your body it just don't seem real.
I feel like Im walking on air,
I love your shy little smile,
The way you do your hair.
Just where have you been?
I needed a woman like you,
Now I know life really is worth living.

I see myself walking onto an open field.
Im not heartbroken anymore
Cause this love feels so real.
How can this be, that only a few months ago
My heart and life felt so empty.
You have me feeling like a teenager all over again.
I'm glad we crossed each other's paths
My dear friend.
I accept who you are, your past life, your kids.
Cause I know you'll return the favor.
I know this relationship can go far.
I look forward to each passing day
Hour and minute.
I'm so happy and in love,
Lifes not worth anything if your not in it.
You're the woman I have forever longed,
Love and admire, you took me when I was broken,
You changed everything
You inspired my fire.

Life's Great

There I sat with my heart broken and vacant.
On this bed of nails I waited for you, patient.
Who was to know everything in life
I would have to lose
To win you in the end?
I lived through a lifetime of abuse.
There was a time when I would only wake
To skies of gray, now they're blue
And all I see and want is you.
Four years of torture and hell,
But who'd guess for you in love I fell.
Gone are the false starts.
Endless tears and broken hearts.
Its never too late,
I'm now in my forties but with you life's great.
I love holding your face in my hands.
I love how youre my last love and I' your only man.
Who cares what my haters say,
In your hands is where my heart will stay.
The scent of your skin, you know the way to my heart,
When you're miles away it always hurts when we part.

My love, my babes, where were you?
I wasted valuable time to the wrong people
Saying, "I do."
But this has got to be fate.
I trust where God has taken me
Cause love with you is great.
Through all the crossroads and windy travels,
We made our mistakes
And into each others arms we unraveled.
At one time I was scared, not anymore.
Im glad I took that first step
And gave love another chance.
I love knowing you're there.
Who would think when I first gave a shy "hi"
To you in 9th grade?
I'm glad I made the mistakes I made,
Cause it made me a better man
To see that life's great.

Ellington

Oh Ellington what memories,

Its where it all started.

Been recently divorced, second time departed.

When in late March right out of the blue

There she stood waving from my rear view

I knew her from high school.

I clearly remember like it were yesterday.

God I thought I got to have her

She's got a style, she's got a way.

We had been talking for a while.

We sat on the bench and as she spoke

I couldn't help myself but fall in love with her smile.

I remember her perfume and her low cut blouse,

she immediately had me under a spell.

I'm not kidding you,

I felt a little aroused.

It was a cool windy chilly night.

I hadn't felt so happy in so long,

Everything about her felt so right..

Oh Ellington, how I would forever recall.

This is the woman I would come to love,

How hard in love I would soon fall.

She was talking about her life, but I was lost.
Where had this woman been?
Why was I stuck with a jealous ex-wife.
Here she was the woman I was looking for.
I know it may seem so soon,
But with every minute, I felt like I wanted her more.
We had already been talking
And texting for a few weeks.
But being here with the person I always wanted
Just what this poor broken down man seeks.
I didn't think I could ever fall in love again.
But here I sat with somebody;
Somebody I had gone to school growing up.
I still can't comprehend.
Who would've thought our paths would cross
Again this time on better terms?
For better, for always, and of all places.
Oh Ellington.

She Didn't Have To

She took in two little girls as if they were her own.
Gave them a new fresh start
And showed them love, gave them a home.
Now their smiling faces adorn her walls,
Two little lives filled when at one time
They had nothing at all.
Just shows you what people do,
She gave all of herself when she didn't have to.
She cried herself to sleep after spending all night awake.
She lost total trust in her man,
And didn't know how much she could take.
So many years of being cheated on
Have left her in doubt,
But her girls finally had that family
So she sacrificed and chose not to get out.
But 15 years had taken a toll.
And she was tired of the abuse.
But she decided to brave it alone.
Her and her babies into the world
Is what she would choose.
Some people take advantage of the good they have
And choose to be cruel.

But still she gave
And gave when she didn't have to.
I needed someone like her in my life.
I was going through the same ordeal.
I forgot how to love, I forgot the feel.
She brought it all back…filled my heart with love
And the happiness I once used to lack.
She believed in me, she trusted me.
When I asked her for us
To start our life together all anew.
She looked me in the eye,
Smiled and kissed me
When she didn't have to.

I Am

I am a father, single parent of a son
And two beautiful daughters.
I am a writer, the company of a woman
And a great lover never a fighter.
Born poor and humble, proud where I come from.
Will defend myself with pen when im ready to rumble.
I am a hard worker, enjoy a good book,
A good movie, especially a good tear jerker.
I am a true believer in Christ,
Believe in true love and always will.
Always believe in happiness and faith.
Leave the past behind you and live for better days.
I am totally devoted to my family.
Believe in forgiveness even to my worst enemy.
I am a dreamer, no matter how old I get.
I know the best is yet to come
Cause I am a true believer.
Music moves me, it takes away sadness, anger.
And even bottled up envy.
I am just a man willing to try.
Not ashamed to love, to laugh,
Lose myself in a good cry.

I am always young at heart.
Look past my age, and inside
You find a shy, playful boy
Not ready to depart.

The Promise

A tiny piece of paper rolled up like a scroll.
I gave it to my love so she could keep it
And always remember and know
Since I've met her, I know its only been five months
But somehow feels like forever
Get her out of my head.
My life has got zero stress.
Told her I'd give her all my love,
That's the promise.
Half a year ago, I wanted my life to end.
Now I cant wait for what tomorrow brings.
Feel like I am born again, like a teenager.
Horny little devil who found his little angel.
Wrote that with me she'll find no better.
I can recite a poem of how much I love her;
Don't ever need a written letter.
And that I'll never love her any less.
Give her my heart, my love, my world.
That is the promise.

How we'll never go to bed mad.

I am so grateful cause she's the best I ever had.

How I will listen, and learn to forgive

Once I wanted to take my own life,

Now all I wanna do is live.

Told her she'd never have to worry

About getting hurt.

Cause I know whats it like to be shot down,

Stepped on, and treated like dirt.

All this comes from heart I must confess.

I know she's not the last woman on earth.

But she's my only love

And this is the promise.

My Greatest Love

The pictures on the wall are yellowing and brown.

About forty years later that young man is no longer around.

So many mixed matched frames.

Lots of familiar faces and many young new names.

Cant believe we're here.

Love do you remember the first time I met you?

Do you remember my dear?

We were two shy awkward kids

But both belonged to someone else.

But how fate would work when our paths crossed

After both our previous marriages would fail.

Remember the first time we touched.

Felt like we were back in high school, like a first crush.

You told me not to hurt you

When in reality I have been hurt so many times

I was scared too.

So glad we took that chance.

We could've missed out on a lifetime of happiness

And endless romance.

So glad we got to see each others babies grow.

All the graduations, all the weddings.

And our first grand newborn.

Remember the first time you cried?
I was there to kiss all your salty tears.
When I cradled your face and promised
I'd wash away all your fears.
Baby after all these years,
I still get butterflies when you walk in through that door.
I could honestly say I fell in love everyday that much more.
Baby I was glad I was always faithful and never lost that fire.
I guess you were always the love us two old folks
In each others arms still full of desire.
Old and slower we would dance
In our empty living room together. Remember?
Now here I lay recalling old memories
Good, bad on what is my final restful day you sit beside me
Still looking so elegant tender and sweet
Your hand on mine.
I remember that spring evening
I met you at that park on Ellington street.
When push came to shove
I thank God your image is the last I'll ever see.
I'll smile and close my eyes.
Goodbye my greatest love.

Her

Her smile.
No matter how dark she can light up a room like a fire.
Her face.
Sunglasses cant hide those tiny dimples.
There is nothing impossible when I'm with her
There is no better place.
Her touch.
When were close that's how I know,
You're all I wanted I need you that much.
Her hair.
Love the scent, love when its all over me.
How it partially hides her face, then its everywhere.
Her skin.
Not only is she sexy from the outside
But she's beautiful also from within.
Her laugh.
When I hear it I think back about how much happiness
And fun we both have.
Her voice.
It calms, it tames me, I put the entire world on mute.
I hear no other noise.

Her spirit.

Nothing would mean much

If I could'nt be with her every hour, every minute.

Her body.

When shes near, its empowering, its electricity.

Her hand.

When she caresses me,

Her touch makes me feel like the total man.

Her lips.

When shes talking to me, I feel myself distracted with them and my mind just slips.

Her mind.

Caring, loving, generous, so much compassion

Truly one of a kind.

Her fingers.

Only one thing wrong.

A ring so she don't get the impression that she's single.

Frankenstein Heart

Frankenstein heart cause its been so tattered and torn.
Been happening all my life.
Couldve been happening when I was in the womb
Probably before I was born.
Covered in stitches.
Loved people I thought I could trust, even married a few bitches.
So please don't hurt me.
Don't add more sadness to my lifetime of misery.
Frankentein heart.
Cause I been called a monster.
Misunderstood cause I always been looking for that brass ring.
That silver lining, that luster.
Seems like I always look in all the wrong places.
Don't seem to find good love only pretty faces.
I know im supposed to be tough, but I'm a one woman man.
Always have been.
Need love not just a pretty face
But someone who is loyal, faithful, who understands.

So please don't hurt me again.

I can promise you all my love

Faithfulness and I can be your best friend.

Frankenstein heart.

All battered and bruised.

Stupid me I needed love so bad I took the abuse.

I hate a broken heart.

I'd rather be dead.

Takes forever to heal.

Temper relief always consisted of alcohol and staying in bed.

But guess what I'm in love again.

This time I hope my happiness has no end.

I cant afford anymore pain,

Or wear another scar

I'm praying all the planets are lined up in order,

Cause Im planning on taking this relationship far.

I hope now this Frankenstein heart can heal.

I hope now that its finally real.

I can feel my heart finally pump and beat,

So please don't burn me.

I've had enough defeat.

When I Die

When I die will the sun still rise?
Will it be cloudy and rain?
Always seems to happen to no surprise.
I know I've seen it in a vision.
I'd die happy not knowing what I've ever accomplished.
But I'd know God's got for me another mission.
Or I think I saw this in a dream.
Probably be crying, sobbing,
Some would probably even scream,
As my casket got lowered into the ground.
I know my soul wouldn't be there
Cause I'd be above you and all around.
Doesn't matter though.
You'd know if you were my true friend
Cause I'd call you bro.
Or you were actually my brother.
Who always saw me invisible.
I was always seen as drama
So I guess they wouldn't ever really bother.

I know I'd be free to look after the people I really love.
To protect and take away all the negative energy.
To bestow love and care for my daughters,
My son, mom, and wife.
You'd know in someways I'll always be there.
I know I'd be the first to say I was never an angel.
I know I did plenty wrong, burned bridges,
And laughed in the face of danger.
But God don't judge by our past.
If you believe and accept Him as your savior,
I'd live in his kingdom of everlast.
I wouldn't ask for anybodys pity or sorrow.
I'd ask everybody to remember my crazy ways with a laugh
And live happier tomorrow.
In my honor raise up a beer.
Hug each other think positive
Wipe away that pathetic little tear.
Remember me for who I was.
Recall my happiness in my final years.
And if I visit you in your dreams, don't be afraid.
Recall the memories, the pictures, the past we both made.
And here I wouldn't be mad
If you forgot to visit my grave.
Cause if I loved you I'd remember
All the good you did everything you ever gave.

People always seem to remember you
Only when you die.
I was no different.
God gave me only one life
And I could say I always honestly did try.

Baby Girl

For Abby

Baby girl just dropping you a note.

Thinking about you miles away

But I cant help but tear up and choke.

Getting ready to celebrate your birth

Many, many moons have passed

Since you've arrived here on this earth.

Little bowl haircut, getting into trouble.

Falling down but always getting up.

Rolls all around your body and chubby cheeks.

My how times passed can't help but get sentimental and weep.

Look at you now, young lady but why do you frown?

Too much on your mind?

Let me share a secret, you and I are truly one of a kind.

You always marched to a beat of your own drum.

You can be stubborn, aggressive.

But in your mind you are never second to none.

I know family life with you was cut short.

But I knew you'd always be a fighter.

That's why your middle name is Hope.

I know your mom and I couldn't get along.

But forgetting the past should only make you strong.

Never be easily persuaded.
Think to your future and your past will easily be faded.
But never forget who you are.
I will always have confidence in you.
You will always be in my eyes, my superstar.
You always made me proud, don't be afraid to dream.
Hold your head up high
Wven if you touch every single cloud.
Someday when your older and I'm gone,
Think about the times we had
Remember me in our favorite song.
Our weekends at the movies,
All the times you cried and confessed your secrets in me.
Don't think of my fails but how I used to inspire.
Don't be afraid of how far you can go.
I'll have wings by then I can lift you higher.
You're a beautiful girl, don't let anybody tell you otherwise
Someday you'll own this world.
Your most powerful tool is your mind, not your body.
Always love, laugh, and forgive.
This is what makes you lovely.
Oh and don't be afraid of making mistakes.
They will help you shape who you will be.
No matter what becomes of your life,
I will always love my silly monkey.

What If

What if you left me tomorrow?
Would all my nights be filled with lonely sorrow?
Would the sun still rise and fall?
Would I be able to see through my tears
And remember the happier times at all?
How would I ever recover, to lose my future,
My true friend, my lover.
Would that song flood my memory back?
Would the heartache be so strong I'd suffer a heart attack?
Would I go crazy wondering who you're with at this moment?
Would he be holding you, kissing you,
Your body, I used to own it?
This could be my worst nightmare.
I could never forget your beautiful face, your smile.
Your warmth, the smell of your hair.
This could be a major catastrophe, honey, baby,
Doll, I couldn't ever imagine the misery.
How could I cope, how would I breathe, wake, sleep, eat?
I'd be at the end of my rope.
Sometimes your still hard to read.
Love, if I'm doing anything wrong,
I'll improve just tell me what you need.

But I know it isn't happening now.
I'm working hard to be a better man.
I'm taking it day by day somehow.
God forbid it ever happen.
I couldn't be angry, I couldn't hate.
All you taught me all your sweetness and love.
I would always relate.
I couldn't ever live without kissing your lips,
Holding you, hearing you, looking at you.
But what if?
What if?
What if?

Spellbound

Here I sit staring at a blank page.
I think about all the things I seen
And how I'm getting up there in age.
Then you cross my mind.
All the happiness I deserved and wanted, I would find.
Nothing is supposed to last forever.
Time is up to God.
But I know He let us cross each others path for a reason.
To be together.
Now I look forward to each waking minute.
You made me feel like a new man,
Deep inside I feel it.
I used to be lost, now I am found,
Holding your face and pulling you near.
Damn, I gotta be spellbound.
I am proud to say I am a dreamer.
I must admit in love I always lose out.
But you have made me a believer.
I am not afraid to fall again, let everyone talk.
I'm happy with my true love, with my best friend.
You're always find ways to inspire.
You light up my life, you always spark up my fire.

With just one look, one smile,
Baby you shine, baby you light up a room.
I get jealous for a minute then I think,
Hell, she's mine.
And that's where my heart races at the speed of sound.
I smile when I see your name on my phone.
Man oh man, that's spellbound.
I laugh when you say you're goofy and ditzy.
That's why I love you, youre real you belong with me.
When I say you're hot, you giggle and shake your head
And disagree with me that your not.
You're everything beautiful from the inside.
You have a kindness you're never afraid to hide.
I want to promise I'm in this for the long haul.
I know times wont always be perfect
But I can gauarantee I'll be there should we rise or fall.
Always with open arms and an open mind.
With every obstacle we encounter,
An opening we will always find.
I truly believe you are my soul mate.
God does do things for a reason.
So yes I do believe in fate.
Ease all the sequence of events that have brought me to you.
Spellbound has me hearing churchbells,
And my shaky voice saying "I do."

12/6

December sixth will be forever in my mind.
I proposed to my girl and in my head I keep hitting rewind.
You see she's just not my girl.
But a special lady who has forever changed my world.
I want to hold her hand as we cuddle on a cold winter
Or in the summer carry her across the beach sand.
I want us both to chase the sun.
To never do anything separately
But to share the same heart as one.
Cannot imagine any waking minute.
Cannot imagine my life without her if she wasn't in it.
Just a year ago I was going through my own personal hell,
But on this night, she made me the happiest man alive.
Cause our love was about to ignite.
Here was this beautiful face looking at me,
Filling my heart with so much love,
And my mind with so much positive energy.
So down on one knee I got down to profess,
I was kinda scared to hear the wrong response.
But to my delight she said yes!
But for a minute though time stood still.
I guess in the moment she couldn't feel.

She forgot to answer.
It was possibly shock
And her body or her mind couldn't transfer.
But this is the woman with whom I want to spend eternity
She makes me happy, keeps me at ease, makes me feel free.
Why live life if you cant live in bliss.
Forever in my thoughts, forever in my heart of hearts.
December sixth.

Birthdays

47 it's how long I been alive
But I could give a fuck.
I'd rather go somewhere and think.
Guess I'll go for a drive.
I'm not one to celebrate my own birthday
Or ask for some time off.
I have been through so much in life
It's the last thing I wanna remember,
Cause I have had enough.
In my life I've gotten used to taking the backseat.
To other men, other dads.
I've learned a long time ago to admit defeat.
My own kids barely remember who I am.
Sometimes I feel to them I am just another man.
Oh well, you get whatever card you're dealt.
I could write till my fingers fall
And nobody in the end will ever care how I felt.
It's just crazy old Jesse at it again.
I can count on one hand who were the ones there for me.
Who were real loved ones and friends.
Oh not trying to be an old grouch.
I love celebrating birthdays for others,

Like friends, family, son and my daughters.
But I hate remembering mine,
Hate remembering age.
Remembering who I am,
Remembering sad times.
At least I got me a good woman who loves me.
But even that isn't for sure.
Maybe I'm just too paranoid, too annoying.
Maybe I'm just looking for more.
But I know life is just a test.
I know I've been through worse.
No matter what, I know I did my best.
But to be honest I am more afraid of being born
Look forward to dying
Than having all these painful lessons I would have to learn.
Maybe that's why I am not afraid of the thought
Of putting a gun to my mouth.
I know it's a cowardly way to go.
But my demons sometimes tempt me
When things start to go down south.
I do try to be strong, find love,
Acceptance from my kids.
Just to get by and the strength to move on.

My real birthday will be the day I take my last breath.
The joy of being accepted into His kingdom
And finally leaving behind my sad mess.
When I finally blow out my last candle on my cake
And the lights on my life finally go out,
Some people will remember my birth
But everyone will recall my death
Cause what I left behind
And what my life was all about..

Invisible Walls

Why is it so hard to open your heart.
We live so close yet are so far apart.
Days may come and days may go,
I dream of forever with you
But I wish you would bare your soul.
Invisible walls they keep us apart.
But brick by brick they will fall.
Sunny days at the coast you held my hand
Never before but that weekend,
You really made me feel like a man.
Oh how I wished I could freeze that moment in time
So I could look back and repeat that weekend
When you really felt like you were mine.
You say you need time to heal.
You have many troubles but I'm patient.
But I want to help cause in my life you are a big deal.
Invisible walls, I can see you but I cant touch.
One day they will fall.
Why do you keep me at bay?
If you asked me to leave I admit I would be hurt,
But I wouldn't stay.

I couldn't live as just your friend or even your ex.
I couldn't exist in a friend zone or even casual sex.
I want more, you had that key to your heart.
Im here waiting, please open that door.
Patiently I continue to wait.
I don't care how long it takes.
I'll count all the moons and stars
Till the day you become my soulmate.
But baby I promise you I am somebody you can trust.
I promise I wont be like all the others, this time it's a must.
I need whats behind your smile.
You're still a mystery to me.
But I love your personality,
Your carefree giving style.
Oh these invisible walls.
One day I'm gonna climb them
And one day I hope I don't die from the fall.

Let Sleeping Demons Lay

Sometimes I feel like I'm not long for this world.
Just when it seems I'm all happy and new.
Out pops the same old.
Sometimes I think what if I died this young?
How would I be thought of?
Like a book that had just begun?
Sometimes I feel like I can speak to you.
Sometimes I feel like you answer me when the sky is so blue.
God, I cant handle another heart break.
Why did you make me out this way?
Why do I keep making the same old mistake?
Why cant I be harder at love?
Why is it when I've found it I cant have enough.
Dear God, dear God, dear God,
What is it that I can hear you say?
Nothing comes easy so lets let sleeping demons lay.
And they come stabbing at me in the middle of the night.
Way underneath my soul.
In the deep bottom its always a fight.
I thought they were gone, long forgotten,
Till I had a familiar spark, heard a familiar song.

They try to push me over the edge.
I can beat them I know I can.
I cant afford to be left a mess.
But something just doesn't seem true.
I don't know if I'm really being loved,
Or just being lied to?
Oh God, oh God, why must you let them stay?
Let them linger, let them sleep, don't wake them!
Shhhhhhhhhh…let sleeping demons lay.

Gold

Just woke up from a dream.
You were four years old and throwing petals into a stream.
Now days I don't know what you're feeling or thinking.
Believe me I regret not being the dad I could've been.
Wish you were still small and things were a lot easier,
When I was your only Superman,
And you didn't feel negative feelings about me.
I wish I could still give you the world.
But I cant all I have to own is that I'm your dad,
And you're my first born little girl.
But I don't blame anyone.
Everything I went through was my own fault.
I lost what I did and everything I had done.
I know your mom and everyone will talk
About my past and irresposibility
But I don't give a fuck.
I'm sorry I failed.
I wish I could've been better,
But that ship's already sailed.
I can't change how you think.
But one day for sure I'll be gone in a blink.

And one day you'll remember me in a song.
You'll regret your grudges you had
And how badly they were all overdone.
I don't ever forget you, I always have you in mind.
I may not hear from you, but I always play that tape
In my head and constantly hit rewind.
Tired of excuses,
And I don't want to make promises I cant keep.
Just remember me in your heart, mama,
And dream of me in your sleep.
Believe it or not, I still keep an old picture of you,
Of how little you used to be.
I cant get over how fast you've grown
And seems like you forgotten about me.
But I guess that's my own cross to bear.
The only thing we have in common now days
Is the last name we still share.
Mija, later on in your life, one day you'll have children,
And become a beautiful mother and a wife.
I hope you still don't resent me down the road,
Cause in everything I been through, and everything I've seen,
In my heart you will always be my gold.

Fakebook

Last night I clicked on that social media site
With the blue screen and white letters.
Been a while but the same drama queen posers
And ruffling of some feathers.
Looks like nothing's changed.
Never missed a thing, never missed a beat.
What once used to be fun,
Now I get easily bored and uncomfortable in this seat.
I used to think and do as everybody else.
Would vent and post personal drama
When my life got bad and all else would fail.
Now as I am growing older or just getting tired of this shit,
You get the same lame people
Taking pics of themselves at the gym like they are all it.
We can only inhale so many pictures
Of your cute kids and your husband.
I am sure you love them.
But that doesn't mean they have to be forced down our throats
Everyday, every minute that I cant understand.
We love making stupid people famous.
They have much more money than you for less talent.
Do you see how lame this is?

I'm just about had enough of this circus.
It used to be so new now I cant get used to this.
Not trying to sound negative cause I didn't click "like it."
Just being honest cause there isn't a button for "hated it."
I honestly think our world and our children would thank us
If Facebook would be forever eliminated.
So what if I got some negative comments
Of some sort of cowardly delivery?
I know who my real friends are.
Somehow I feel it wouldn't really matter to me.
Wont also be a hypocrite.
Just gonna be less in it cause I'm tired of this shit.
For now I'll just stay away.
Maybe write another book,
Maybe cruise off the seashore,
Never better than being misunderstood.
More time to be real, more times to be with the ones I love
And less time to be on some Fakebook.
Unfriend me if you want.
Some stuff is not meant to be kept personal.
Cant put up with scrolling
Along another selfie in some restroom.
Your in line at a supermarket?
Could care less where you shop or at so fuck it.
Take me off your list.
I don't care if you wont read what I write.

But you are curious and you'll be pissed.

Go ahead and post another pic of your food.

Cause you know we are all dying to know

What you're gonna eat.

Yea people are gonna be rude.

Its what you get when you put yourself in that position.

Pick your REAL friends wisely.

With social media,

Modesty is permanently out of season.

Nuthin Else Matterz

Been a year since I been with you.
Lately all my dark skies and lonely nights have been clear blue.
Its been a long road for the both of us
Lots of things we had to recognize.
Our past relationships have left us with a lot of hurt
And a lot of lies.
But I want to promise you I want to make right.
I try my best everyday, but I wont lie,
Sometimes its like a fight.
But you are worth it "D."
You're worth going through Hell for.
I'd do anything cause nothing else matters to me,
And feel you next to me when we sleep.
I dream of an eternal life with you.
I pray that someday you accept me fully and one day say, "I do."
But I am learning to be patient.
I'd rather lay forever on a bed of nails
And wait than have my heart vacant.
Just to see you smile and your gentle caress.
I'd hate to imagine a life without you,
Damn, I'd be a total mess.

I'm sorry if sometimes I come as jealous.
It is so unlike me,
But I can never picture you with another fella.
I just have never loved another woman like I have loved you.
If you ever quit and asked me to back off,
I would if that's what it came to.
I apologize for whenever I hurt you.
I cant stand my image.
I walk around breaking mirrors.
And all it takes is for you to hold me
And talk to me and I get those familiar feelings and shivers.
I confess I still get the bitterness
That makes my stomach rumble.
All it takes is one look
And I get weak in the knees and I stumble.
Its been one year, I may not have the history with you,
But I am grateful to have walked into your life
And loving you now and loving you here.
All the trials and tribulations, meeting your family, friends.
Loving your kids and all the happy relations.
But baby, I know you're still scared.
But what would life be if you had never givin me a chance?
You'd lose out on a man who really loved you.
And really cared.

I know its hard to fight your fear.
But imagine what life has for us around that corner,
Beyond that one year?
But I love you so much I would give you up,
If that's what you wanted.
I couldn't imagine the nightmare if we ever parted.
My heart would break like glass
With a million pieces shattered,
But I'd do anything for you
Cause nothing else matters.

Madre

Like a flower growing in a dessert you endure.
The love you've shown, your love is real,
Your love is pure.
Oh mother, may I just say, "Oh my how time flies."
Your tired eyes have seen so much pain.
Decades have passed but your love is still the same.
Your hair has turned silver and gray.
But you'll always be beautiful to me
And in my heart forever you will stay.
Your words are sometimes sharp.
But your soothing voice is like music to my ears
Like an angel playing a harp.
Your wrinkles on your skin, nut you're strong.
If people knew how hard you fought and where you'd been.
They don't make women like you anymore.
I get a pain in my heart everytime I walk out your door.
I dread the day you will no longer be alive.
But through my heart and blood and veins
You will always thrive.
One holiday can never be enough.
Cause you define strength, perfection, trust and love .

Oh mi madre mia,

Con mucho amor para siempre en mi Corazon,

Desde el premier dia.

Graveyard Of Broken Hearts

I think I'm finally convinced I wasn't meant to find love.
It seems when I find it, I get that ever familiar shove.
Why even try, why even move on?
I feel like that poor shmuck everyone writes about
In a sad love song.
I envy those that true love they finally find.
How do they do it?
And when will it be my time?
Not in this lifetime I guess.
I am meant to roam around lonely and sad and a total mess.
I have nothing to call mine.
Only my hopeless dreams of love
And plenty of worthless writing time.
How do some people get that storybook life?
Like in the movies, with the happy home, kids.
And a love-starved wife?
Oh well who knows?
Not me, not I.
Some people always get the roses
I get the thorns.
My love life seems a revolving door.

If people only knew how much I could offer.
I'm so ready to give, to love, to bring happiness.
To offer so much more.
I'm tired of waiting for my chance, the fairy tale,
The love, the endless romance.
I don't want to try again once Im alone.
I'm done, this time for sure, I mean it till the end.
Cause I don't wanna fall when my happy ending starts.
I'm getting used to being a ghost,
Rattling my chains in my graveyard of broken hearts.

After The Fall

So what becomes of us after the fall?
Thought you'd always stand by me,
And I'd always stand tall.
I find myself on familiar ground.
If another heart breaks in a forest does it make a sound?
I knew one day it would come to this.
Hopeless dreams of sugar kisses and fantasy wedded bliss.
Oh well too good to be true.
Couldn't force yourself to love me,
But I'd cross the world twice for you.
I over flowed my cup till it spilled.
When I found you I thought my cracked heart was finally filled.
Think I met you 20 years too late.
Think 20 years ago I definitely would've been your soulmate.
Promises never kept, shattered hopes and sleepless nights
On a soggy pillow from all the tears I wept.
Kindred spirit and always a true friend.
If I was reincarnated I'd come back as your lover
And do this all over again.
In the meanwhile I'll never hate you, I never will.
It'll hurt to think back on those memories
And I'll be loving you still.

Lucky man whoever gets to love you next.
I just lost concentration thinking of you.
I lose focus.
I cradled your heart in my muscular arms.
I cradled your face and promised you
I'd never do you any harm.
Wish there was a way you could make it clear
And explain it all.
Wish there was a way you'd catch me,
So I wouldn't hurt after the fall.

Created To Be Hated

It's been a long road or so it seems.
Used to be I could do anything.
But now when it comes to failing, I am king.
Oh brother, why do you ridicule and laugh at my misfortune?
It wasn't that long ago that you yourself
Wwam in that same ocean.
Oh yes let the world criticize this bumbling clown.
I've fallen oh so many times, but here I am still around.
Kill them with kindness they say.
But with each word it leaves a scar.
And that's where it will forever stay.
Yes I am human, I do hurt.
I put on a brave face and try my best to make my life work.
Its always easy to judge my poor descisions
Without walking in my shoes.
Thing is I risk anything, take a chance win or lose,
It's all right to put all the blame on myself.
Don't hang out with family,
Cause I feel like a hypocrite, an empty shell.
They say blood is thicker than water.
If that is true why is it that people you are born with,
Make you feel like you're the only black sheep out to slaughter.

It's ok though I wasn't always like this.
Once had it all, but I couldn't see.
That's the man I don't really miss.
It's so much easier to swear at me and shake your head.
I've made a lot of mistakes.
I guess you can say I made my own bed.
Yes it's my own cross to bear, oh my brother, my friend.
My cousin, one day I'll cease to exist
And I no longer be neither here nor there.
For your pleasure I shall fall flat on my face
Every now and then.
Don't need your pity and act like you care,
Only to laugh behind my back again.
In the end though I'd rather die a poor man,
Without a penny, rather than to pretend to be arrogant,
Rich, two faced, full of resentment and envy.
Life as it is way too complicated.
Not trying to sound paranoid, down and negative,
But truthfully, in a way, I was born to be hated.

Battlefield

Looking back my life resembles a battlefield.
So much has happened.
Can't separate what is fake from what is real.
Bodies strewn everywhere.
Broken hearts, scars.
And I even grown white and gray on my head of hair.
So many battles fought.
Looking back now I think they are pointless,
But the real reason...I forgot.
So many disputes unresolved, friendships, marriages,
Even brothers in my eyes dissolved.
I stood for what I believed but most times I got beat,
Burned bridges, made a bad rep.
But like a man I took my own heat.
What was the point? Nobody won.
You can raise your flag all you want,
People know the truth nowhere to hide nowhere to run.
Abrasions, scrapes, and only bruises, in family and love.
No matter what weapon you choose, everybody loses.
Love is a battlefield, yeah Pat Benatar said it.
Been through it all, like everyone.
But damn, I loved to regret it.

Like warriors we all survived the battlefield.

I look today with souveniers.

Bring all my memories full of fears.

Its all the blood I've shed.

all the careless egos I've fed.

But I've put all my past troubles to bed.

But out on this battlefield,

The demons keep laughing in my head.

Mirror, Mirror

Mirror mirror why do these things

Keep happening to me

Mirror , mirror is there such a thing as being happy.

Is there a big great target engraved on my heart?

Why does this world spin better when I'm falling apart?

Mirror, mirror is it true

That all that glitters isn't really gold?

Mirror, mirror I finally want to find true love

Cause I feeling I'm much too old.

Just when it seemed

I had the whole wide world in my hands.

You slipped away and through my fingers

Like grains of sand.

Mirror, mirror why cant you make time stand still

So I could freeze that moment I met her,

Instead of reliving the day my heart got killed?

Mirror, mirror I know

I may not be the fairest of them all

Mirror, mirror I always manage to dust myself off

Everytime I take a fall.

God help me breathe new life from within.

Help to overcome this rapture in me
Oh, this tortured sin.
Why must I surround myself
With other hurtful souls
Who are full of poison and so fake?
I fall to one knee with the pressure
But my heart shivers and aches.
Mirror, mirror what if this is just one big fairy tale?
And I am waiting for my princess to arrive?
Mirror, mirror please wake me!
Tell me this is real and that this time
She isn't carrying a knife.

Smile

My job sucks.
My boss is a prick.
somedays I just wanna fuck this and just quit.
But instead I smile.
My co workers are all drama and talk smack.
I swear people are immature maybe from the brains they lack.
But still I manage to smile.
My car just left me stranded guess.
It finally took a shit.
I swear a normal man would've gone insane and had a fit.
But my faces still manages to creep up a smile.
No matter what curve ball life throws at me.
I always manage to leave with a shred of dignity.
I know the good Lord has got my back
No matter how many wolves in sheeps clothing
Come up to attack.
I am an Olympic swimmer in this sea of life.
I smile to myself and fantasize.
That life is good no matter how bad.
Cause I know God has given me the best I ever had.

Just today I got paid and my check is a joke.
But hey, you know what, I am alive and at least I aint broke.
In my heart I am the richest man alive.
I am all love and faith and with that I smile and thrive.

Raise My Fist

I raise my fist, when times get tough.
I say a prayer when I almost give up and I cant resist.
When I want to quit, all the times I wish I had a gun.
Cause that's all I wanted to do is say that's it.
But I don't, and I wont, no matter how things get worse.
I pray to my Lord cause I know he's got better for me
Than a ride on a hearse.
So what if more times than not I was dealt a bad hand.
I always did what I could at the end of the day
Cause in the end I am just a man.
I raise my fist, when life wont give me an inch.
I try to grow stronger, I persist.
I admit more often than not I get lost in my own pity party
Sometimes I wish things were different
And someone loved this nobody.
Most days I just lay awake at night, and think how tired I am
Of the struggles, tired of the pain, tired of the fight.
I don't know what's kept me alive.
Maybe the good Lord wants me to be 92
To tell my great grandkids how I survived.
No worse nightmare than having no one love you.
No kids visiting, no honey to hold, no one there

I try to be strong, everyday I battle my demons
But somedays I don't know how long.
I count the stars in the sky
And pray to God when will it be my turn to fly.
Don't get me wrong I try to stay upbeat.
I have always been a warrior and can't admit defeat.
Meanwhile I raise my fist
Cause surviving is the only thing on my bucket list.

On The Real

I layed awake one night whispering why God why?
And He said just sleep my son, lay back.
It's not your time to die.
But once I sleep my memory runs wild like a movie reel
Flickers and flashes of painful and happy moments
And even things that looked so unreal.
Jump out of bed and pray as I kneel
Try to find the answers
To all the little mysteries in my life
But man oh man on the real.
So many puzzles and riddles I just cant understand.
Was I cursed for the way I was?
I could've been more honest, a better man.
But life deals you many twists and turns.
Many friends I still have and many I know I've burned.
I'm done with the blame
Cause there's always three fingers pointing
Right back at me
And the more things change
The more they stay the same.

My life turns like a broken old wheel.
I've paid my debts,
Punished for my past ways
But man oh man on the real.
Been betrayed from the worst,
From my father to my brother.
Wish I could've had a better relationship
With my son and my daughter.
I am grateful that when I wake to a better day.
I think of what is in store.
I thank my Lord as im on my bed a smile and lay.
Who knows
What the next twenty four hours will reveal?
I'll leave it in His hands
Cause this old dog has seen worse.
But man oh man on the real.

If You Ever Have Forever In Mind

I thought better things were supposed to come
To those who waited.
Maybe I'm too old.
Maybe I took too long.
Maybe long ago I hesitated.
I didn't know you then
But I wish I had.
I was too busy starting on my own life,
Dropping out of school, getting married,
Being a young dad.
If I had known you existed,
If I were single then I would've reached out
Cause our love would be too great
And intense to be resisted.
I'm sure its not your fault.
I'm sure it was beyond your power.
I'm sure you got tired of waiting
For your prince on his white horse.
I got tired of rescuing fake princesses
From prison towers.

Somehow I lost the key
To everything I needed to find.
Then comes you and you've had it all along.
And I wonder if you ever have forever in mind.
I've never seen myself as a prince.
More like always the frog.
Not being negative.
Just so used to lifting my head up so high
Above this fog.
Sometimes when we fight I feel
Like I can see the end.
Then you reach out for me
And its beautiful to begin again.
I don't always know where this path will take us.
But I do admit without you I feel lost.
I cant predict the future or whats down this road.
But I'd love to hold your hand
When I take my last breath when I am gray and old.
Every fairy tale has to someday end.
Just tired of what I been through.
Felt like I had to pretend.
There's special people you meet in a lifetime
And you are that kind, Honey.
I'm here waiting if you ever have forever in mind.

Glimmer and Fade

Today I died, lived my whole life
Not knowing I was living a lie.
Ok, so I was only dreaming.
Sometimes it feels better than really living.
The pains and struggles of life get far too real.
Most days I am immune to hurt and just forget how it feels.
I honestly wonder how long I have to hold on.
But I guess it's not for me to decide.
Only God knows how long.
When the time comes and I start my journey to embark.
I wonder what I will leave behind,
What will be my mark.
When my last tear drops, my last beat of my heart.
My last breath leaves my body.
I imagine the splendor.
I imagine if I touched a thousand lives
Or maybe just one somebody.
I've always heard what shimmers isn't gold.
Looking back I have always been a spark,
A tiny glimmer and now I am fading to old.

Cant ever do like Christ and stretch out my arms.
Somehow I felt I always wore a crown of thorns
And that's been doing me harm.
What will I miss?
So many I dissed.
An unfinished bucket list
Wrapped in a tortured pain I possess.
Under it beats a heart tattered, torn and left a mess.
I walk across a graveyard and feel blessed
Af what life offers to gain.
I gently touch each tombstone and think
No future equals no pain.
Used to be loud and boastful
Then today I am more toned down,
Slowly my glimmer has begun to fade,
So says this mask that wears this frown.
Sometimes I find myself twisted
With so much jealousy and hate.
Wonder how long my candle will glimmer before it fades.
I close my eyes and everything goes black.
Only this time when I wake I wont be coming back.

Two Little Girls

Two little girls.
Two little girls that I have come to know.
Two little girls that I've had the privilege to watch grow.
And whenever I do or if I ever don't.
They'll always remember
That my love for them was true.
Two little girls know that I am not their father.
Yet they know I love them immensely
As if they were my true daughters.
I don't ever pretend to ever take the place of their dad.
But I am there to provide a hug
When their day has gone bad.
One little one and one older sister.
Both curious but the little one
Has the chubbiest cheeks you cant resist her.
Inseparable wherever they go.
They miss each other when one isn't there.
They're blessed with so much love.
They teach me everyday on how to care.

Two little girls who know how much
I love their mama.
But they are forever my girls.
I couldn't imagine ever going home
And not listening to their little drama.
Both spontaneous and full of energy.
They bring happiness
And complete our little family.
They remind me what its like
To be a dad all over again.
I don't ever want to wake from this dream.
It feels so real there is no reason to pretend.
It's an inspiration that sends my world
Into a whirl and swirls.
There's these two little reasons:
They're my two little girls.

#NOTENOUGHHOURS

Not enough hours to count all the stars in the night sky.
Not enough hours to listen to your heart beat next to mine.
Not enough hours to spend with you.
Not enough hours to daydream of the day we say "I do."
Not enough hours to protect you from harm.
Not enough hours to find excuses
To just hold you in my strong tattooed arms.
Not enough hours to make you laugh as I sing you a song.
Not enough hours to prove to you
I am not like the other guys; you've still got me all wrong.
Not enough hours to caress you and pull you near.
Not enough hours to try to cheer you up
And capture that rolling tear.
Not enough hours to regret the times I made you upset.
Not enough hours to make love to you, and oh?
What was that fight about?
Oh well I forget.
Not enough hours to never take you for granted
And cherish every waking moment with you.
Not enough hours to be with you every day,
And never grow tired of seeing you and loving you.

Not enough hours missing you
Even when you are sitting across the room.
Come here, sit next to me.
Lets get away together.
If not tomorrow then soon.
Not enough hours in each single day.
Honey I'm sorry this was so long
But it comes from my heart.
Every word that I had to say.

Thorns

Thorns.
That's the way my life has been from the minute I was born.
Don't need to bitch,
Don't need your pity,
But if I had to choose between life and death,
I'd rather dig a ditch.
Throw in all my troubles and sorrow.
Drink a shit load of booze and not even think of my tomorrow.
Fuck all the memories I used to adore.
I'd trade this baseball cap today for my crown of thorns.
That old black and white photo album don't mean shit.
I have a brother that stabbed me in the back.
Uno dos tres,
Too many times that damn prick.
Learned a long time ago not to believe in trust.
My own father betrayed me
My hurting my own daughter in a blind fit of lust.
Ok, whatever mama.
I am tired of turning the other cheek and ignoring all this drama.
I feel like I am falling into the same bush of thorns.

I try mama, look at me, mija.
Believe me, I want the halo.
But all I keep feeling are these horns.
I just want peace.
To be alone with the real people I love
And all these wars in my mind to cease.
One day into the future I'll be underground.
Wouldn't care who pisses on my grave
Cause I'll be at rest rocking with God,
Not even hearing a sound.
You live and you learn,
But in the end you come out battered cut and bruised.
Bloody from all the thorns.

Music

Song in my head, lyric on my mind.
A at the tip of my tongue, a rhyme.
That's my life inspiration.
Everywhere I get on that bus
Headphones on and the music takes me there.
Get up every morning , bones cracking, muscles aching
To a job where little money I am making.
Music inspires my soul when I am depressed.
Worried or happy, I turn it up and just let go.
Splash cold water on my face.
Get into my beat up old car,
Put on a country station
And it takes me to another place.
I love all types of music.
If it's got a story and it moves me then I use it.
On the bus I close my eyes and drift away.
I am swimming in a sea of musical notes
On my way home after a long hard work day.

So many songs of yesterday

Remind me of today.

Got a ton on my mind.

Music calms this savage beast

Then I have nothing left to say.

Brush my teeth

And I crash straight into bed.

Say a prayer.

Headphones on.

Go to sleep with a song in my head.

Oh Sister
For Ashley

Did you watch that shooting star last night?
Thought it was you.
Had a dream two angels whispering to each other
So I guess it must've been true.
Gone too soon they always say.
Wake reliving those painful final moments of that day.
The pain grows heavier in my heart.
I feel it will never go away.
Oh sister, was that you standing over me
As I slept the other night?
Something about your presence
Made me feel so safe and so right..
Wind blowing your hair on your face,
Sitting in front of the bonfire there
Couldn't have been a better place.
Special moments like these were never enough
Looking back at pictures when we were younger
Who would have thought your life was going to get so tough.
But you fought with the heart of a lion.
Your bright smile and your blue eyes light up my horizon.

Tender moments that that I seek,
In the stillness of the night in my mind
I can almost hear you speak.
Of the crying, the timing
And how it looked like we had it beat.
A part of me believed it
Cause you didn't know the definition of defeat.
Lonely walks on the beach
As I watch my baby play in the park.
I know she sees you.
I think I saw you push her on the swing.
She was your heart.
Been months now, oh sister.
Could be million of years and I'm always gonna say,
Oh how I missed her.
Did you watch that falling star last night?

Angies 20th B-day

Pretty smile.

Big eyes for this once young daddy.

What a wonderful surprise.

Wiped that little butt and those tiny tears.

My oh, my has it really been twenty years?

Seemed like only yesterday.

Playing with your Barbies

And dragging around your Winnie the Pooh out to play.

Falling off your bike.

Little ballerina dancing across a big great stage.

No matter how old you'll always be my baby at any age.

Lifetime

Met the most beautiful girl today, mama.
I need to see more of her.
If I have to marry her, I'm gonna!
I even see her in my sleep.
She dances across my mind.
I love caressing her little face even when she weeps.
You've gotta see the way she cares.
My heart melts with her tender touch,
And oh the way she just stares.
She's prettier than any picture I've ever seen.
I know I'm awake but scared it could all be just a dream.
I can make her happy I know I can.
She turned this graveyard back into a garden
Inside of this old man.
You gotta see how she loves her children.
How she puts everyone else first.
She is my never ending glass of water
Cause all this time I been dying of thirst.
She's my queen, my princess.
Lover, friend, and everything else in between.

Sometimes I can read the stress on her face.

She don't like to worry me

So she just smiles, and in that instance

She lights up the whole place.

May never get the chance to give her all the money and gold.

But all I have is this hardworking man,

Faith and respect till I take my last breath

When I'm gray and old.

Mama, met the most beautiful girl at the park

And we had wine.

She asked if I'll always love her

And I replied, "Yes. A lifetime."

Hey Dad

Hey dad feel like I don't know you anymore.
Seems like everything got so different
Since you been behind that convalescent room door.
Used to admire you, you were my hero.
Just the way you used to work.
Days and nights on a tractor.
Used to come home scraped and scratched,
And all covered in dirt.
Hey dad, even when you left us, and mom had to carry the load.
I'd pray to God to bring you back home
And walk back down that familiar road.
And when you came back
It seemed like a happy home once again
But there seemed like something lacked.
Seemed like something in you would change.
You became distant, darker, and had a little rage.
Hey dad, I know it was hard living with you at home.
I know the day you hurt my daughter,
I wanted to tear you flesh from bone.
But Mama stood between us.
Losing respect for you that day was a great loss.

Hey dad, I'm older now

And I've learned to forgive and forget.

All the pain you caused in my life.

Life is too short to live with regret.

And even though you've never come out

And apologized and remained as stubborn as a mule

I just wanted to say...I still love you.

You did teach me to be a hard worker.

And you know what? I'm not sad.

I wear those scars of my youth like a badge of honor.

Just wanted to say, hey dad.

And I don't visit you much, you seem lost.

You don't talk so out of touch.

My heart feels heavy.

I hold so much back cause, I understand your situation.

But in me I try and pray to let go

Of all this unwanted resentment.

Hey dad.

Chapter 3

Woke

The painful lesson I learned after my last relationship ended is fully experienced in this final chapter. The agony, the signs, the hardship I not only experienced from her but to be honest the stress I too brought to her. The heartbreak was the deepest here; loss of jobs, dishonesty, and finally betrayal took my mind in overdrive to the brink of suicidal tendencies. Struggles got worse. I lost everything.

But I saw the light of truth through my losses and the rediscovery of myself and faith once again in God.

In the end I hold no resentment regardless of what you'll read, they were merely lessons that I take with great respect with the person I shared all this with and who still holds a place in my heart. Always.

Fieldworker's Son

I was born a fieldworkers son
Moving from town to town
School to school
Kinda messed with me being young.
But mom and dad worked the fields.
They built their dreams on blisters and tears.
Dad brought mom over from Mexico.
A wide eyed innocent girl.
Her dreams of America
Would forever change her world.
Her petite body would change over the years.
Childbirth, bruises and scratches
From the vines and branches of working the fields.
The image of my mom running through an orchard
Pulling hoses with sprinkler soaked wet in the morning
Hours on a winters chill
Picking grapes in a dead heat
While the boss man overlooked from the patio
Of his mansion sipping wine
Still makes me ill.

I can still smell the fresh tortillas
And hot beans at 4:00 AM in the air.
Mama made a killer lunch
No matter under what tree I sat,
Dirt or splinters, I didn't care.
Being out there at my young age
I couldn't see myself doing this all my life.
But to mom her prince charming made the fields
And made her his wife.
But daddy worked hard
To give us new shoes and clean underwear.
He never believed in hand outs
Or uncle Sam's welfare.
He'd ride that tractor from dawn till midnight.
He'd come home covered in dirt.
Scratches on his face like a boxer
After a championship heavyweight fight.
Even after dad left us
Mamma continued to work her fingers to the bone
She couldn't speak English
But taught herself to drive
Just to get us to school and give us a home.
Even after dad came back,
Mom welcomed him with open arms.
She always taught us never to return the harm.

Oranges, cotton, or grapes through all the drama.

My folks stuck it out through all the seasons

Of love and hate.

Till dad went to live in the hospital

And mom had to retire,

They instill memories to this day that I still admire.

Today as I speed on the freeway rushing to work

On my usual morning run.

I glance over to see people

Hunched over picking fruit.

I think to myself proud to have been

A fieldworkers son.

Writers Block

Writers block, staring at a blank page
Far from home, people supposedly miss me
But I suddenly don't give a fuck.
There are people that I really miss though.
But have grown leery and less forgiving
Of those guys who call me, "bro."
Miles are just numbers,
I forget them after a while
Like a whore forgets her lovers.
Tired of the life, tired of the work.
Gotta keep everything inside.
Tiptoe on eggshells for fear of sounding like a jerk.
Writers block, miss when I was younger.
Didn't have the goals, the responsibilities, or the anger.
Why can't life be like a movie or a T.V. show.
After a half hour everything is happy, back to normal
And we can just go.
Work all the time, wish I could see my mother.
Hug my children.
Wish I had a dime.

The harder I work the further I get.
Getting too old to worry about my mistakes
And past regrets.
Writers block, I can complain all I want.
Drink all I want, and piss away all my damn luck.
But the more I worry about feeling so stressed.
The more I see the few people I still love
And cant help but feel so blessed.

She Is

She says she isn't pretty anymore.
I say, not true.
Why does my heart skip a beat
Every time you walk in through that door?
She says she don't look or feel young.
I say stop it, every time I listen to music
You are in every lyric, every artist every song.
My princess, my love you are my confetti on my parade.
My love, my gorgeous
You are all over me like on a hot day.
You are my ice cold lemonade.
She says she don't look sexy or nice.
I say oh quit it, cause every time I look at you
I still get butterflies.
She says look at all this gray.
I say oh my, my, my you look sexier to me
With each passing day.
In my house of life she is my foundation
My reason to strive to do better.
She is my love and adoration.

She is the rain on my face.

The beautiful girl who walks in and lights up this place.

She Is my partner for life.

I don't need to marry her to trust her.

I love her, and call her my wife.

I wipe away a tear from her as she whispers, "I believe you."

I tell her "You're so much cuter when you smile,

so quit being so blue."

I hold and kiss her hand, and whisper in her ear,

"Its an honor to stand by your side and be called your man."

Broken Man

I remember being young, so full of energy.
Empty dreams but nowhere to run.
I remember being in my mother's arms.
Always felt safe cause my dad was tall, strong,
Ready to protect us from anyone
Who would threaten us with harm.
Fast forward, and I'm a broken man.
Paying all regrets and the fires I started
And flames I had fanned.
There are people out there who think I love the abuse.
They keep thinking and judging
Cause they've never walked a mile in my shoes.
But I listen but never retaliate.
I let them seal their own fate.
Life has taught me to absorb their hate.
But in my mind there exists a tiny typewriter.
Cause silently I am writing lyrics and words
Cause mama never raised a quitter
And life's taught me to be a fighter.
They see a broken man but I find inspiration,

Through their negativity I use my pen.
That is my ammo and words are my poison,
So fire without hesitation.
And even my kids have left me on the ground,
Dying and bleeding.
How quickly they have forgotten.
The ways I've fought and lost.
Cause of them and I never end up winning.
Family has kicked dirt in face and mouth.
Many moons ago I sacrificed for family.
And raised little humans.
And now I been ditched like a broken old bike
In a dark corner that nobody cares about.
Like the land of the misfit toy, I am a broken man.
But God, I miss being young
Running outside on my bike like a little boy.
I remember looking in the mirror and telling myself,
"Look at this man, he's so broken."
Then a voice says, "No you're not."
I turn around and ask why?
My beautiful lady places her hand on my chest and says,
"That is me in your heart, I am helping you fight.
I am the voice in there that just has spoken."

Live For The Memories

They say blood is thicker than water,
But to me you don't need to be blood to be family.
So that saying to me don't really matter.
I surround myself with people who love me.
For who I am, they don't judge my past,
Or the once upon a time broken down man.
They're the people I fight with and die for.
If your gonna nitpick and criticize
Just cause we grew up together
Don't even come around my life anymore.
That's the reason I wear that tattoo of a bleeding heart
Behind my right ear
Just a reminder of hearing the negativity
From the people I used to trust and the their shit I have to hear.
Now I live at peace that I have detached from my past.
That sad, cancerous disease, these people are my family.
We camp, go on trips, argue, have dinner.
But for the most part we live for the memories.
So if you come to analyze stop that pointing finger
And remember there's three more pointing right back at you.
Don't believe your own lies

So let us be.

It's not with our eyes but our hearts that we see.

Jimmy is my brother, Deanna my partner for life.

These two little girls are my babies.

Think twice about hurting them

A I'll come after you with a knife.

We don't worry how tomorrow is going to be.

It's the moment right now

Music, love, laughter,

And we live for the memories.

Can't Sleep

The roses are red.
The violets are dead.
The demons run circles
And do jumping jacks in my head.

Mama Cried

Blocked my brother today, from my phone
Possibly from the rest of my life.
He has been circulating awful words
To hurt me in the worst of way.
He and his wife, he's threating me with violence.
I am not afraid,
I actually pity him, embarrassed for him.
So I reward him with my silence.
He wants me to be confrontational,
But Mama would cry
And I cant stand to see that old lady so emotional.
Last time I saw him I was helping mama move
And he dropped by not saying a word.
Later that night he texted me attacking my friends
And me for helping Mom.
Felt like I wasn't with a knife but with a sword.
Cowardly you may say?
Betrayed by you again.
In another time I'll forgive you my brother
But not today.

You have everyone judging me by my past
Again and again.
Brother, cant change what I did,
Who I hurt, or who I burned.
I was a different man back then.
You stir my demons like a glass.
You force me to drink.
I'm older, wiser, with scars and blood on my hands.
And crosses to bear.
I've totally renovated the way I think.
You said when you see me in public
You want to fight.
Again there's no fear.
Aint got nothing to prove.
Just in my heart I know you are not right.
People tell me, "Bro, he's your blood."
I say that's ok, more power to him
For thinking he's a bigger man
For dragging me through mud.
Deep inside I feel like shit
Cause I wouldn't want my kids
To do that to each other.
So really I am just being a hypocrite.

And mama still talks how tight we used to be.
People used to think we were twins
And she laughs at our younger years.
Then she stops, cries and mutters.
"But all now that remains of my life,
Is a trail of tears."
I can't help it, Mama, I tried.
All for your pride.
All for your selflessness.
All for your stubbornness.
All worth it to think..Mama cried.

Queen

Its not the way I planned to be.
Me staying home unemployed
And her getting up to head to work at 7:30.
But my honey, my baby, my love she rocks.
Even when I am stressing pulling my heart out,
Thinking, damn, my life sucks.
Her smile lights up a room.
Her tears fall like the rain.
Her positivity hides her inner gloom.
She fights to make others happy
As her stress and her fears fill her brain.
I try to ease her tension.
Rubbing her feet and an ear to talk to as another layoff
I had that I regret to mention.
She is the most beautiful person I have ever met or seen.
Yes sometimes we fight, but at the end of the night
She will always be my queen.
I know she deserves better.
She may have wished meeting a more successful man
But never a minute goes by that I regret her.

Through her smile I see the worries in her eyes.
I daydream of being super successful
And giving her everything her heart desires.
Her not ever working hard is what I fantasize.
Her sexy silhouette fills the room through the moonlight.
She readies herself for bed and for a minute
Everything in my world is right.
Most times we hardly make love or even touch.
It's okay I understand.
Just feeling her close to me and listening to her heart beat
Just means so much.
She carries the load.
If she were a rainbow,
At the end of it she'd be my pot of gold.
She is my princess my fairy tale story at the beginning,
Fills my book with happiness, sadness, and love
All the way to the happy ending.
She is my queen, morning noon, and night.
She is always my everything.

Random

I have lived a life.

Boy have I lived.

I have cried.

Man, a river I have cried.

I have loved so much it hurts.

A thousand times I think I could've died.

Just when I am about to quit cause my life is a mess.

I look around at my people

Who love me and whisper to myself,

"Shit, I am so blessed."

When I'm Gone

Watch the antifreeze sit on that table
And I want to take a sip.
How do I keep getting dragged into this mess?
I am so sick of this shit.
Recently seems like I can't do anything right.
Every time me and my girl are alone,
It turns into one big fight.
But damn it I try, I even made friends with her ex.
I lay awake at night thinking how did I get into this mix?
I don't know shit gets easily confused.
No matter how I say it, someone gets offended and I always lose.
Tired of this same song.
Will anyone remember me when I am gone?
She is so quick to point out my negative but not my good.
Whatever suits her is fine I always got to give into her mood.
Like I think why am even around?
I seem like a burden.
Yeah, just roll your eyes.
Cause I always seem to bring people down.

But I do try to think of happier times,
Like our days out on the coast,
Beautiful memories.
I miss them, but they are just a shell an emptiness;
A ghost.
She wont even look at me.
Not even a smile or a touch.
Guess I am yesterday's news.
I guess I don't mean as much.
One day the world will get a shot in the arm.
Cause they wont have me to kick around.
They'll miss me when I'm gone.
Most days I just want to sleep and never wake up.
But I guess God needs me around cause I am so fucked up.
But I just want to be done.
Sick of the pain, sick of the pretending.
Cause I know nobody will miss me when I'm gone.

Toxic People

Toxic people since the day we met.
That will always be a day I will soon never forget.
I remember that day, I remember that night.
I also remember that feeling,
But I didn't see was the cancer had slowly and quietly set in.
Our good times we would cherish would be memorable
But also be minimal.
But the people who wouldn't leave us alone
And constantly interfere would be criminal.
We were toxic to begin with.
What had started as friendship would end with a poisonous kiss.
Why did it have to start like this?
Why did it have to end like that?
She was my dream, she was my world.
Didn't she know I needed her bad?
But we were both toxic, but I didn't care.
I threw my hands in the air and I said fuck it.
We had pasts that hadn't yet healed.
But together we felt high, drunk, and everything spun so unreal.

She was my cocaine but I was her straw.
Without each other we had lost everything.
But together we had it all.
Toxic from the very start.
What was promise and passion ended with a dagger
And an overdose of a broken heart.

Fools Gold

You hurt me so bad.
I wanted to take my own life.
Cause you meant that much to me that bad.
I hurt you too after you had kicked me to the curb.
You moved in my own friend.
And I couldn't overcome how that was so absurd.
You had brought so much joy and pleasure.
I felt like I was a deep sea diver
Who finally found that beautiful sunken treasure.
Once upon a time I thought I was too old.
I had found love once again,
But once again it turned to fools gold.
But yes to your credit you had helped me when I was down.
When I got laid off you helped turn my life around.
But the break up did a number on my mind.
I saw you getting closer to my own friend.
I slowly felt I was losing my beautiful one of a kind.
You kicked me and my 73 year old mother to the cold road.
What was a 24 karat love turned into that moment fools gold.

You thought you had rid yourself of that cancer.
You were so proud of yourself but you had no answer.
I did what I could do on a poor mans salary.
I know I wasn't heaven to you,
But damn it you were the moon sun and stars to me.
I spoke to someone else after we broke up.
You hooked up with my own friend
While I still lived with you.
But I'm the one who fucked up?
You, my ex friend, and your ex husband shaved my beard,
Cut my hair of my head.
Humialated, embarrassed, dragged through the mud
And left for dead.
Didn't matter I was still a friend to you even after.
But can't still forget how in the bitter end
You still chose him.
And I'll never forget his mocking me on the phone.
And his laughter.
I thought finally my empty heart was sold.
You proved otherwise.
And that was the end of this fools gold.

Backseat

Who'd had thought what you would do to me.

What was a dream come true

Turned back into my nightmare and my misery.

If I had known what was to come,

I'd had put a stop to our relationship before it had even begun.

But I took a backseat to both of your ex's

And I stayed cool.

Then you became close to someone I used to call a friend,

I have nothing but hatred now for that fool.

What can you see in him when he is half your age?

I feel disgusted, betrayed and just filled with rage.

Yet you deny he's your lover.

Why not just admit it?

I have seen the evidence.

He's young enough to be your son's older brother.

But like a man I swallowed my pride and stepped aside.

And admitted defeat.

Guess wasn't bad enough all our 4 ½ years

I always took the backseat.

Never would I had put you in the same situation.

But you always proudly catered to your ex's from day one

As I was neglected and just wallowed in my new infestation.

God, girl, I worshipped the ground you walked on.
But we couldn't ever have our day in the sun,
Unless they too always came along.
Just once would I had loved the scenery from the front view.
Just once would I had loved to see where life
Would've taken just us two.
But it bothered you that I showed a hint of jealous.
You are lucky I was respectful.
Any other man would've gone insane
And caused all kinds of malice.
But I was the one who took your ex into our home.
I quickly became the outcast, the stranger.
I found myself begging for attention.
Scraps. Not even a bone.
Never did you realize just what you had.
I even worked hard at becoming a good step father
To your daughters much better than their lazy dad!
But I guess its true.
Good guys never finish last.
We couldn't had a future
Without you always focusing on your past.
All that loyalty and faith I showed you over the years,
You accused me of betrayal after we had broken up
And out came the sorrow and your tears.

So after you kicked me to the curb,
I started months later talking to a girl.
You claimed I should've told you,
But you were the one who shit on my world!
It was deja'vu all over again.
Felt double-betrayed all at once by the woman I loved
And someone I used to call a friend.
But that's fine, I survived and I took the heat.
I shall rise once again and learned a lesson
To never again take a backseat.

Father's Day

August 4th will forever be etched in my memory.
That was the day God took away my father from me.
Don't even want to care all the wrong he had done.
I, myself, was no better.
But I was proud to be his first born and oldest son.
He came from nothing at all,
But we never worried about shelter.
Cause he always provided a roof and four walls.
He stood tall and never asked for hand outs.
You never spoke much but you taught me to work hard,
Cause that's what life was about.
Yeah, I know growing up you caused mom lot's of pain.
We drifted apart as I grew.
I never understood the animosity of so many things
I can no longer explain.
When you finally went into that nursing home.
I rarely visited.
But when mom could no longer drive,
I took her as she constantly persisted.

I am glad she did though,
Cause in those last few weeks I got to know you better.
I became closer to you and I guess better late than never.
You never apologized but I saw the sorrow in your eyes.
I knew then you were destined for paradise.
I saw mom break up
As she knew she was about to lose her long lost love.
I knew at that moment really soon.
They'd be calling you from up above.
And even as I saw doctors and nurses
Run in and out of your room in a frantic,
I thought I had prepared myself,
But I fell to my knees and cried in a senseless panic.
I feared for my mother,
And held her quivering body in my arms
And at that moment I hoped I was also closer
To my estranged brother.
I took one last look at my poor withered father.
Where he would last lay, kissed his cold forehead
And held his once strong hands,
And remembered how this is now my father's day.

I Remember...

I remember your smile.
I remember knowing you from school.
But damn, that's been a while.
I remember meeting you again on Facebook,
But seeing you in person was different.
You were more beautiful, you past your stories, your look.
I remember us sexting each other and daring each other.
You sounding so tough, but after our first sexual encounter,
We were addicted like teenagers we couldn't get enough.
I remember your harsh past, how he hurt you.
How you needed to get away.
How you wanted me to be your last.
I remember how you made me feel.
Like I was special, a rock star, a prince,
A fairy tale come true everything was so unreal.
I remember your family, your kids, your friends.
How everyone wanted you to marry me.
I remember our fights, all of a sudden you were unsure,
But I couldn't sleep till we made up and we were right.
I remember losing my job, I felt like less a man.
But you helped me up, you paid my car.
You still had so much love.

I remember you wanting us to end.
I still wanted us to try.
But I lost so much sleep.
I tried to imagine all this was a nightmare
And we were just playing pretend.
I remember you moving to work up at the coast.
I remember missing our date nights.
Our cruises,
Sex,
But most importantly missing you the most.
I remember you moving in my old friend.
I remember looking into the future
And predicting our dreadful end.
I remember the pain, swallowing all those pills,
Not wanting to wake cause I knew nothing again
Would ever be the same.
I remember, I remember, I remember.
By damn fucking God I remember!
I remember that spring of 2013.
I remember your smile.

Oh My Brother

Oh my brother thinking back when we were young.
Playing in our room listening to radio any old 80's song.
Building roads with our hands for our hot wheels.
Who'd ever thought many years later
I'd find out what a knife to the back from you would feel.
We'd talk about girls
And what a mystery they were to you and me.
Who'd ever thought one of them would tear us apart?
Anger, bitterness and envy.
Oh my brother, I know I was far from perfect.
I ruined relationships.
Burned bridges through dishonor and neglect.
You always made sure to remind me of my struggles of my past.
Oh my brother, with each passing year, we only get older.
And I wonder how long this can last.
I can never wish you any harm or ill will.
Yet you've threatened me with violence and surround yourself
With a woman with a forked tongue and looks that kill.
Been years since we hung out.
You hardly say anything when we cross paths.
But once my back is turned
You're quick to cast doubt.

Oh my brother this is why I faded and laid low?
Got tired of the talk, and cheap shot blows.
I don't think I am better than anyone.
Did a lot wrong, lost a lot too.
But never forgotten where I do belong.
My path has been hard, painful and long.
But I don't need you to criticize and cut me down.
I'll have God to answer to when I am gone.
Oh my brother you laugh when I fail or fall.
Your bitterness and hate get the better of you
When I am doing good and standing tall.
You throw shade and kick dirt in my face.
No matter the hurt, I'll hold in my heart for you
A better place.
You hurt the people I love when you brag and you boast.
I shake my head cause I know it is not you.
The brother I respected is but an empty ghost.
Oh my brother thinking back to when we were young.
Hot wheels, action figures, girls, and old 80's song.

Tidal Wave

A tidal wave of emotions.
Felt like I was just hit.
But now I've grown tired of being weighed down.
Negative and depressed and feeling like shit.
Realizing there is more to my life that means too much.
The love of my grown children who never gave up.
My faith in God means more than any woman's touch.
I am putting confidence back into my life.
No more hurry to find love, or looking for the next ex wife.
I know I am a good person deep inside my heart.
Once upon a time I wanted to end it all.
But today I'm hitting restart.
I am a beautiful person, I am learning to love myself.
I am learning to be good friends with the man in the mirror
And everyday I never stop rehearsing.
I am learning to trust in God
And the few people who really love me.
Done on waiting on that person who broke my heart.
She's merely now just a faded memory.

I don't hate her, I actually thank her for trying to fix this man.
But when you really love someone,
You neve quit.
You only fight everyday to understand.
But today I am better than that.
Got me a new lease on life.
Walk around with a strut and a tip of my hat.
I wake up with a smile and God pumping through my blood
That tidal wave of emotions
Has now turned into a powerful positive flood.
I have been forgiven.
Thank you, God, for getting me past that last chapter.
I am grateful cause here I am breathing and living.
I will never forget those loyal few
Who always believed in me.
And just gave, gave, and gave.
I am high fiving you all as I grab my surf board,
Cause honey no longer am I drowning.
I am riding this tidal wave.

Sacred

Sacred is my heart.
Been lied to carelessly and shattered many times,
Broken and shredded apart.
Sacred is my life.
At one time I didn't value it
Cause I was so devastated in a relationship
Where everything turned into an endless lie.
Sacred is my love.
I know I deserve better
And when I find her and my time is right,
I will be given more than enough.
Sacred is my time.
I have no patience for lies
Nor do I need to rant.
But I will always have the time for rhyme.
Sacred is my faith.
I talk to God and he guides me through this life of a maze.
Sacred is my mother.
Most days we don't see eye to eye.
But God only gave me one
And she gave me life
So there is no other.

Sacred is my small circle of friends

Who are heaven sent.

They help me smile, love,

And keep me from going hell bent.

Sacred are my children.

They are my world.

They have followed me from every bad relationship

And every move in.

Sacred is my success.

Nothing came easy

And couldn't be possible without the struggles of my past.

Working hard, holding on,

And dreaming have made me blessed.

One Day

One day I no longer will feel this pain.
I'll be able to wake to her image and not want to go insane.
One day I'll be able to love again.
I'll be able to trust love without worrying
About being backstabbed by a friend.
One day I'll be able to smile into the mirror,
Look positively into the future
With 100% full of hope and glimmer.
One day I'll pick up my broken pieces
And not feel so wrong.
I'll pick myself up, put my chin up,
And once again be strong.
One day I'll be able to forget this nightmare,
Go on with my day like I used to without a care.
One day I'll learn not to make the same mistake twice.
Sometimes being naturally kind comes with a heavy price.
One day can't come too soon.
Believe me, I'm a positive person
But somehow can't shake off this never ending gloom.

Jesse Gonzalez Jr.

One day I'll be able to look up at the sun

And not be blinded by the light.

I have my good days but most times it's a constant fight.

There will hopefully come a moment

When I'll be able to give my heart away.

Sadly not tomorrow, not soon.

But I pray one day, one day.

Kingdom

Behind the eyes and smile
Lies a tormented soul who lives near a river of tears
That circles around my kingdom of denial.
On the outside I look alive,
But inside my hope, dreams, and happiness
Live on top of a house of cards
I had at one time built up so high
And now its about to take a dive.
Oh great man in the sky,
I chuckle to myself.
What obstacles will you have me climb today?
Please fill in on another lie.
I think I'd be missed by some.
But I'd be lost running in my forest of doubt
Swimming in my pool of pity,
And sitting alone in my dark castle inside my kingdom.
Why do I continue to stall?
My demons tempt me to take two steps forward
But I take two steps back, hoping for a miracle.
But I am too tired.
Maybe I should just take the fall.

The jobs don't come, the money is gone.

And the kids don't call.

I've seen some glory days.

So I sit and contemplate on my throne in my kingdom.

Cant even give my girlfriend her glass slipper.

This prince has turned back into a toad.

I can only give her love, but she don't return it,

Cause even she knows I cant be the man to help her.

Somewhere there is a dusty old noose.

Living my life has been difficult.

But my kingdom calls.

Don't know how much longer till I have to choose.

Feel sick and numb.

I've run out of tears like I've run out of excuses.

The sun don't rise and fall and I feel no pain...

In my kingdom.

#Fuckit

Don't write for the fame, or the recognition.
I will always be who I am and stay the same.
Live by my own beliefs, my own faded image.
And my own definition.
Don't do it to put a dime in my pocket.
Releases stress.
And to some poor fool out there who just may relate,
Fuck it.
Never cared to be a glorified school jock,
Over-credited book worm,
Mr. handsome popularity.
I guess that's why I'm paying for it now.
Cause back then I didn't give a fuck.
One day I know I'm gonna shine.
Could be tomorrow,
Next year or maybe never.
I used to blame others but not no more,
So when it does come
That glory's gonna be all mine.

I keep praying to my God.
I don't know what bad I did him,
But whatever it was, that invisible man I pray to
Leaves me in this never ending fog.
But oh well, that's my own cross to bear.
My own personal hell.
Keep writing to keep myself at ease.
Don't feed me your empty sympathies.
Just leave me alone please.
I always do the best I can.
In the end I made my own bed.
I was weak, negative.
Just a man.
With a pen, paper, and an empty wallet.
Got my own dreams, dark thoughts, prayers,
And two tired, broken middle fingers.
So fuck it.

The Year

So as I sit and recall the passing of another year.
I can't help but feel somber
And can't still believe I made it here.
Lost the love of a woman I cherished and adored
For almost five years.
If I owned a canoe I'd paddle across my own river of tears.
From all the begging for her I did.
The painful secrets and the sadness in the back of my heart
That I once hid.
Alone again in my apartment
As I fall into a heavy slumber.
I recall that fateful day
I lowered my father's casket later that summer.
And all the negative thoughts I still try to steer clear.
Oh man I still cant sleep from thinking of that dreadful year.
Lost another job or two.
Got backstabbed by a young friend I once knew.
Forgot where life ends and where it begins.
I tried suicide and was reminded
Ot was one of Christianity's greatest sins.

Well fuck, guess this damn year didn't bring me much luck.
Cried as I stared at my 23 year old daughter's old baby pic.
Sat in my car and drank half a bottle of Jim Beam.
And nearly choked on a bottle of pills till I blacked out,
Cause they made me sick.
Moved my mom out of state.
Fighting loneliness and these thoughts of envy,
Jealousy, and hate.
This was truly a year I wont soon ever forget.
Cant go back and erase all the stupid things
I would forever regret.
God, I remember starting the year so happy.
Now I fight and pray everything the devil has done to me.
But it's a struggle to keep my head positive and clear.
But I got to keep fighting, hoping and praying I make it.
Cause hey, there's always next year.

Wish I Never Knew

Wish I had never peeked behind the curtain.
But I was young and confused about love
And things then were a little uncertain.
Wish I was still young and dumb
When I could easily shrug everything off and carry on,
Iinstead of breaking down every time
I hear her name and oh that song.
I wish I had never found out so much.
Now I know the secret to the magician's tricks
And how I constantly crave a woman's touch.
Felt like love was similar to the wizard in Oz.
So much fantasy and fairytale
And really there wasn't much to all the fuss.
Try not to think of the pain but the feelings run too deep.
And those scars behind my heart
Of blissful memories I still keep.
Kind of regret finding what love was.
Cause now I'm drained , saddened, and total loss.
I envy him, wish I was in his shoes.
He's such a lucky guy
Cause here I sit daydreaming of her
All battered and bruised.

He's so lucky he gets to kiss those lips.
I feel so stupid reminiscing,
But I used to be him,
And my knees grow weak and my mind slips.
I sigh, but I'm barely breathing.
Yes there's more to life than just a stupid heartbreak.
But I feel like I can't get on with this stupid healing.
Wish I never knew about love.
Thought it was like in the movies.
Romance and happy endings.
Not like a drug you can't get enough of.
He's so lucky he gets to touch her in ways I used to do.
Stupid memories keep running though my head
And each passing day they keep running through.
Wish I never knew, if time could turn back.
When I was nine and my heart never wondered
And I never grew.
He's a lucky man.
He's probably putting a ring on her finger now
And promising her memories that will last.
While I sit in an empty apartment
Looking at pictures and living in the past.
Wish I could wake up with amnesia and I lost my memory.
Falling in love hurts.
I'm a repeat target.
Live with regret...just look at me!

He's so lucky he gets to see her everyday.
Meanwhile I lay awake repeating our break up
That fateful sad day in May.
Wish I never knew,
But one day may take years.
But God will point me in the right direction,
And this time I'll know what to do.

Book Of You

World at your feet.
If I were reincarnated,
I'd look forward to the day again that we'd meet.
Thing's didn't go exactly as planned.
I thought you'd be forever my love
And one day I would take your hand.
Don't need to get into the dirty details.
We cried and hurt so much.
No matter how hard we tied everything fails.
I have to get used to being without you.
But cant help it going to kill me,
When I see you with someone new.
But all our tears have reached the ceiling.
A part of you will forever live in me.
And my heart will forever have a huge empty feeling.
I have to put old memories away that haunt my head.
I need happier thoughts so I can sleep instead
Of laying awake at 3AM,
Tossing and turning in my bed.

I remember our last kiss.
The feel of your body,
The scent of your skin.
And your smile and laugh
Is what I'm going to miss.
Someone else who is younger
Is making you happy.
I can't hurt you anymore.
No more stressing and living in misery.
If I were to be selfish, I'd force you.
I wouldn't be happy though,
Cause I know what we had is gone
And that wouldn't feel true.
I wrote half a book about you.
I found inspiration in us.
You brought life into me
And I loved everything that we used to do.
But I now need to be the better man and walk away.
Used to believe you were always my tomorrow
And my fresh start and my new beautiful day.
I need to close this final chapter on this book of you.
I thank you for coming into my life
And making everything old feel like new.
Peace and love always be blessed my friend.
In another time, in another life, in another world.
May we meet each other again.

Lost

For just once I'd love to be lost in someone else's eyes.
I want to be swept away by true love and not lies.
Want to go on an unplanned road trip.
Wanna play radio deejay.
Sing lyrics and act goofy till time just slips.
Not even remember our destination,
Buy meaningless souveniers and junk food
And snacks at a random gas station.
I want someone I can lay at night and count the stars with.
I want to know someone is crazy in love with me
And can't stop chewing on my lips.
I want to be the first thing on someone's mind when they wake.
I want to be the last thing at 3AM that keeps them up
No matter how late.
I know I may sound like I'm speaking a foreign language.
I have been through so much hurt.
I want to find real love cause it has yet to be established.
I feel my heart will turn to rust.
I want to know what's it like to be loved and feel lost.
I want to know what's it like to be someone's M.C.W.
I want to hear her scream,
"I fucking love this man, I'm so into you!"

I want to be the reason you circle a day on your calendar.
I want to be the reason I go through great length
To recue my princess from any prison tower with my ladder.
One day I intend on lifting my head from this fog.
One day I for once want to play the prince
Instead of always the frog.
I want to be the reason your friends giggle
About your smeared lipstick
And on you the scent of my cologne.
I want to be the reason you sleep on my side of the bed
When you are alone.
I want know what it is like for once
To be truly wanted before I die and turn to dust.
I just want to know what it is like to be someone's reason
To be in love and just in my heart get lost.

Beautiful Day

You were like Julia Robert's in "Pretty Woman."
I don't know what the future had in store for us.
But on the horizon something was always looming.
You always figured breaking up was the answer.
But not a day enters my mind and its slowly away like a cancer.
T-shirts still hang from the times we used to live in your trailer.
Out on the coast, our pictures still hang staring back at me.
Frozen now; they're just ghosts.
Too much hurt and painful memories
You can't help but retrieve.
Part of me agrees,
But a fairy tale ending I fool myself to believe.
Sometimes I feel when the memories die, I will too.
I can't help falling apart.
You were my everything
You were my glue.
All alone I fall to pieces.
Everyday it gets harder but I try, boy do I try.
I pray endlessly to Jesus.
There's got to be a cure for this broken heart of mine.
I've heard all the advice yeah, yeah, yeah.
It takes healing and time.

Don't get me wrong, I do have my good days,
Some hobbies and T.V. shows
Take momentarily my heavy heart and dismays.
Some friends say she just isn't worth it.
Love to see a beautiful day bro.
But how can I when I imagine someone else loving her
And it makes me feel like shit.
I need to find a way to remove this pain.
Cause everything else fails.
I get lost in thought, or see old images on social media.
And I lose it and cry like hell.
Drunk with memories of that sad ending in late May.
My eyes are finally heavy, I'm drowsy, pills are all gone.
As the bottle hits the floor, no more hurt and agony.
At last a beautiful day.

Villain

Been called worse.
Bad people with bad vibes gravitate towards me
Like a bad curse.
Burned bridges with people I've only known seven weeks.
Some people are fast to judge my mistakes.
But when it comes to my good deeds nobody speaks.
Women I thought were friends
And just turned out to be ho's
Friends who have backstabbed me I once used to call bro's.
Been said I'm like all the other men.
I do have heavenly thoughts but I cant help if I look like sin.
I swear I don't mean to be stereotyped a villain.
I pray exceedingly to God to help with my spiritual healing.
I need to find my focus again.
Need to stop this trend of fake relationships and just find friends.
I need to find myself, need to end this villain rep
And put heart off my sleeve and back on the shelf.
I need to find what it is to make me good.
Need right people, right timing, right religion, right mood.
They say nothing good is meant to last.
Youre telling me I need to slow down,
Live for just me and quit looking for love fast.

I say I don't care what people think.
But truth be told I do care.
Need to stop looking for answers
At the bottom of every drink.
Life will be good when I finally find my place
And am just chilling.
I wish to someday put everything behind me move forward
And recall I once used to play the villain.

After The Fall pt2

What becomes of us after the fall?
After we've climbed every single mountain
Now here we are with nothing at all?
Empty walls where pictures once hung.
Painful reminders of you in every single lyric, every single song.
My heart has bled every drop
Has been sucked dry.
We've turned every page, every corner.
You cant say we never tried.
Who knows what becomes of us.
I am sure you'll prosper.
I'll never regret you, you'll always be a beautiful loss.
You'll always be my favorite mistake.
I'll probably hear your name in the air
And a smile I'll have to fake.
My heart will hurt at your mere presence in public.
All our memories will flood back
And in that instant I'll whisper,
"Why did our love have to be so tragic?"
I'd hate to imagine your sails will find a new wind.
I'll imagine holding you next to me.
I'll ignore my tears and force myself to mend.

Letting go was probably the hardest thing I ever had to do.
They say if you love someone, set them free.
But I don't think that's ever true.
Who knows where I'll be after the fall?
Nut you're a beautiful soul, no regrets, no nothing.
You deserve to move on to better and stand tall.

One Thing

If you could wish for one thing what would it be?
To finally escape work, ditch responsibility and finally feel free?
To never have to pay bills?
To give your strength to someone you love
So they relieve their ills?
To finally thrive?
To spend a vacation running on a beach
With someone you love and so happy to be alive?
To lose weight?
For just once to watch the news
And not have to see any politics, greed or hate?
What would it be? What would it be?
To end all wars and let everyone believe in peace and harmony.
Just one thing
Could change everything.

Wannabe

I want to be loved.
Not just loved but adored.
By a woman who cant get enough of me
And who always asks for more.
I want to be looked at at as someone
Who has just won the lottery.
Someone who loves every scar.
Every flaw, every inch of me,
Wannabe loved for my body
And respected for my mind.
Someone who constantly compliments me
And tells me I'm their one of a kind.
Someone to hold hands with at the fair.
Ride or die kind of chick,
Who runs their fingers through my dark black hair
Someone who wont hurt me again.
Total trust, confidence, no other man.
Just a best friend.
Want to be a rock star in someone's eyes.
Want to put my heart in someone's hands
And not to be afraid of games or lies.

Someone who looks at me with full of desire,
Sparkle in their smile and in the bedroom, fire!
Mostly I'm tired of being alone.
Tired of being hurt.
I want to know what it's like to taste heaven
Instead of always eating dirt.
Envy watching guys happily holding hands
With their girlfriends.
Sigh and wonder what it's like.
That will never be me.
They're so lucky
Maybe one day,
Maybe I'll always be alone till the end.
Wannabe loved.
Not just be loved, but adored.
Tired of sleeping with nothing.
I want to know what it's like
To go to sleep with more.

Battered

Battered from pillar to post.
I've taken my bumps far more than most.
But here I still stand,
Just a shell of a once prideful, happier man.
I am so torn.
Curse my folks for ever having me.
Here to suffer.
Should've never been born.
These last few days have indeed been dark.
Feel like I'm at the end of my rope.
Think I've lost the will to fight.
Feel restless, about to lose all hope.
Just tired I guess of my life being so predictable.
I am a raging war inside
And I want to do the unthinkable.
But I haven't got the guts to pull it off.
Fed up with life being so God damn Rough.
I really hate sounding like a pity party.
But I wear a mask with a fake smile.
Just to satisfy and fool everybody.
And seriously everyday doesn't even bring any change.

Feel like everyone just tolerates me
And forces to love this old battered three-legged dog
Covered in mange.
Tired of excuses and complaining.
Tired of silently crying.
Tired of being judged and criticized
So I just keep quiet.
I wouldn't hurt a soul, so instead I hurt myself
And relish in my own personal riot.
I am beyond help and beyond repair.
I've let the ones I love and even my enemies
Have their way with me.
I just no longer care.
Let everyone be loved.
Let everyone be more popular
And march down their own parade.
I'll just stay here in the background.
It's what I am used to and eventually I'll just fade.
I've forgotten what its like to be alive for so long.
I have been bruised and tattered.
The feeling of being invisible and neglected
Has been so common.
No other way for me to live
Than to accept being battered.

Last Day On Earth

Last day on earth whatever shall I do?
Heard an old friend took his own life.
God bless him, he's a lucky fool.
Wonder what went through his mind
In those final hours.
All the contemplating and thinking and fighting.
Unforeseen powers.
I do however feel his pain.
A muted cry for help.
Losing your grip on everything
And nothing else to gain.
My last day I will be scrolling
Through old pictures on Facebook.
Reminiscing of happier times with people I used to love
Just take a final sad look.
But the pain and betrayal runs deep.
Those same people I still love and they are the reason.
I stay wide awake at night and lose so much sleep.
My last day, I think I'll be listening to music
And drinking some beers.
Maybe say a couple of prayers and talk to God.
And even shed a ton of tears.

I think by now I probably cried a river.

I know what I am contemplating

May not be the answer,

But I've read our God's a forgiver.

My last day I think I will throw me a barbeque.

The smell of food in the air, maybe it will be nice

To have one last happy moment.

God knows I've had a few.

That used to be my favorite pastime.

Cooking, music, playing with the kids.

And the woman I used call at one time mine.

My last day I think I will go for a long park walk.

Watch people play with their loved ones,

Laughing and playing and loving

And just be numb to it all

Cause I no longer give a fuck.

Think back to my first day on this earth.

I had no choice then.

Hate to say I do now, but I am done.

I need to spend my last day on earth.

She's Gone

You got your hand on the door.
I turn away as you wipe away a tear
And you look down.
I look back to you
But the door shuts and you are no more.
Under which rug were all our good memories swept?
Traded all for fights and secrets we both kept.
Hate the feeling of being all alone.
Just want to get stupid drunk.
Till I cant feel the heartache.
And how low this pain has sunk.
I miss your scent, miss your feel, miss your song.
Should've begged harder, cried longer
But she's gone.
Our last fight was the worst she cussed me off.
Once upon a time we were rolling around
Looking into each other's eyes.
True love...but I cant blame her.
She grew tired of trying, too much crying.
Too much lying.
And deep down I cant stop from dying.
She's so beautiful.

I envy whatever man's arms she lands in.
What a wonderful new beginning for her
That can only come from our The End.
She's got the whole world at her feet.
I have nothing.
She was my world, I sit alone at the table
And next to me where she used to sit
An empty seat.
I know eventually I will survive.
But feeling wanted by her made me feel so alive.
I told her I would wait for her no matter how long.
It may take forever.
I may have to eventually face reality.
Cause she's gone.

Here Lies A Man

Here I go looking for the next great verse.
But no matter what I write,
Everything comes out like a curse.
A double edged sword, people get hurt
And start to bury me
And send me out on a hearse.
Everyone seems to be a critic, but nobody is a fan.
So goes my story so says my tombstone.
Here lies a man.
What will anyone remember about me when I'm gone.
A man who worked hard,
Tried to do good,
But in the end all he ever did was wrong.
All I ever wanted was to be loved.
Tried to do well even to the ones who didn't like me.
Tried too many times to turn the other cheek.
But always to be met with misery.
So much for well-laid plans.
So says my tombstone.
So it says, here lies a man.
But I was grateful for the good times I did have.
Little romance, little adventures, some laughs.

Tired of tip-toeing around eggshells.

I want to write about my life,

But I don't mean to hurt anyone.

Either way, no matter what, I still get hells.

Life is too short to stay bitter, so I've been taught.

I quit keeping track of the heart breaks

And all the wars I lost and fought.

I rack my head thinking,

Of ways to write the next great American novel.

Nobody takes time to read my work.

They're too quick to label me a hater

With a poison pen and a shovel.

Don't be too quick to kick my face with sand.

I only wrote what I felt and in my eyes witnessed.

So here lies a man.

Girl With The Broken Smile

She's so pretty.
She used to be mine.
I was happy not too long ago,
Once upon a time.
But she didn't want to continue.
Wouldn't give me a choice.
Ran out of excuses.
Didn't get a second chance.
Didn't get a voice.
She could've lost her smile
Long before I met her.
Must've been when she was younger.
Must've been her broken trust.
Im not too sure.
But if she wanted me back,
I'd do it in a heartbeat.
All the painful pasts all the painful memories
I would delete.
I wouldn't mind starting all over again.
Cause waiting on the side lines sucks.
Being just a friend.
So there are these moments

Where I just want to caress her
And touch her lips.
But she pushes away.
And I forget that it isn't like it used to be.
And my mind just slips.
I guess it's mostly my fault.
Wish I could redeem myself
But she cant recall all the battles for her
That I fought.
I look at her as I drive, she is quiet.
Looking straight ahead, lips pressed.
Man this relationship used to be so alive.
Even through her sunglasses
I can read her mind.
These drives used to be filled with laughter
And conversation.
Wish I could put everything into rewind.
See that girl?
She used to be mine.
I felt proud.
I was her only one.
Her sparkle in her eye, her one of a kind.
You see that girl?
She used to want me.
I wasn't always invisible.

But now you can literally see right through me.
You see that girl?
Yes its been a while.
She used to love.
She's so beautiful even with her broken smile.

Just Saying

When I was here I had a super power.
I was the invisible man.
Now that I am gone from here everyone misses me
And I want to be seen.
When I was here I was easily neglected and tolerated.
Now people cry for me and speak of my good moments.
I had no idea I had any moments.
I was so accustomed to laying awake at night
Worrying and thinking and crying myself to sleep.
I regret what I did, but I cant change a thing.
I went too far, too late to turn back.
When I was here I only wanted to be loved,
And wanted instead of being told I am annoying
And I suffocate people, and I am too pushy.
But now they want me back?
I was treated like a child.
Better to be seen and not heard.
But I am here, standing next to you
And they still cant see me.
Maybe cause they are too busy crying over my shell
And laying flowers on my stone.
Theyre too busy praying.

I wish I was there to comfort them

And care like I used to.

But I cant find my way back.

Just saying.

Feel It

I party like a rock star, but I aint got no money.
Dress like a pimp but I aint got no honeys.
Crave on sex like a porn star,
But im not always horny or own a sports car.
I write like a rap star,
But I aint got no gold.
I can feel it.
I am still young but I feel too damn old.
Days rumble on and I still wake alone in my sheets.
Waste too much time thinking
And less time falling asleep.
I need a change that'll never come.
So I daydream with alcohol in my system.
Till I'm all numb.
I am a pirate,
But I haven't found my treasure chest.
But no matter how hard I try
I never do my best.
Feel like a cowboy but never owned a gun.
An erect penis whose fixed and no desire to cum.
But yet I feel it, that desire to break that glass ceiling.
Any day any minute.

It's only a matter of time I guess,
Before I strike gold and I am famous.
And out of this mess,
A sniper who cant hit his mark,
A dog whose forgotten his bark.
A car with no D to move forward.
My knees are so scabbed from falling and yelling,
'Oh Lord!'
A T.V. with no remote,
A cruise ship with no life boat.
But yet I wake in the middle of the night.
And I feel it.
I splash water on my face and I pray,
"God help me get over this shit..."

Paisa

Paisa?
Why, cause the color of my skin
And the sound of my speech?
How ignorant can you be?
Is this your intelligence?
Is this what they teach?
I am proud of what I am from,
I love my stars and stripes
But I don't hide like some.
Call me paisa,
But I was proudly born here.
Joke if you must.
Got Mexican blood running though me.
Proud of my folks
I ain't got no fear.
All my life I was labeled a wet back.
But I keep quiet
Cause I know they are afraid of my knowledge
And that is the intelligence they lack.
Paisa cause of the way that I speak?
Yes I can't pronounce most words properly
Cause of my upbringing.

Categorize me all you want but your judgement is weak.
So my parents weren't born here in the U.S.
Doesn't make you better than me.
Cause yours were and I know any less?
I am proud to call myself an American
And make the best of what I got.
Proud to be a part of this great country
And support the freedom my forefathers
And the wars my brothers fought.
Not angry or bitter.
Actually makes me chuckle to be judged.
I let them think they are better.
Paisa cause of my last name?
Ok, pretend to be a gringo all you want
But your heritage tells me you and I are the same.
I will continue to embrace my history.
No longer ashamed like I was when I was a kid.
I am just proud to be me.

www.ingramcontent.com/pod-product-compliance
Lightning Source LLC
Chambersburg PA
CBHW050624300426
44112CB00012B/1650